Cooking with Soy

Cooking with Soy

NEW
HOLLAND

Yoshiko Takeuchi
photography by Sherly Susan

4822029

First published 2013 by
New Holland Publishers Pty Ltd
London • Sydney • Cape Town • Auckland

Garfield House 86–88 Edgware Road London W2 2EA United Kingdom
1/66 Gibbes Street Chatswood NSW 2067 Australia
218 Lake Road Northcote Auckland New Zealand
Wembley Square First Floor Solan Road Gardens Cape Town 8001 South Africa

www.newhollandpublishers.com
www.newholland.com.au

A record of this book is held at the National Library of Australia and the British Library.

ISBN 9781742572604

Publisher: Fiona Schultz
Designer: Annie Pearlman and Tracy Loughlin
Editor: Jodi De Vantier
Photographs: Sherly Susan, www.sherlysusanphotography.com
Food stylist: Yoshiko Takeuchi, www.healthysoycooking.com
Assistant chef: Rie Sakata
Hair and make-up artist: Lin Ravel (profile photo)
Production director: Olga Dementiev
Printer: Toppan Leefung Printing Ltd (China)

10 9 8 7 6 5 4 3 2 1

Keep up with New Holland Publishers on Facebook and Twitter
www.facebook.com/NewHollandPublishers

Thanks to:
Noritake for crockery and glasses page 4, 44, 45, 48, 50 (glasses), 53, 59. 62, 63, 73, 82, 83, 84, 85, 87, 92 (tea pot and cups) 101, 112, 120, 124, 125, 131(big plates), 138, 141, 161, 176, 189, 192, 193 (tea set) 198, 202 (front cups, oval plate) 217, 225
Spiral Foods for providing quality products for this book.

Noritake
Japan 1904

My hope is that this book will inspire healthy living.

May this book be helpful and useful to those who would like to increase their plant-based meals for ultimate health, those who have diet restrictions because of allergy or disease and those who gave up or are trying to give up animal products because of their love and care for animals and the earth.

Let's enjoy cooking and eating even more!

Contents

Introduction: Why cooking with soy?

I have always believed that what we do in this world should reflect our greatest passions.

I love food and I enjoy anything to do with food; not only eating and cooking it, but also learning about food and its nutritional benefits—even shopping. I also enjoy sharing recipes and passing on my cooking skills. That is why I have been a chef for over a decade and have taught cooking for nearly 20 years, both in Japan and Australia.

I love almost all foods, but I have a special passion for tofu. There might be food out there that is tastier than tofu and some people think tofu is bland and so avoid it. But tofu is a healthy food—it is low in fat and calories, has zero saturated fat, it's cholesterol-free, rich in protein and provides bone-healthy minerals, like calcium, potassium and magnesium. The benefits of tofu are many and easy to find.

I have a strong passion for health and place a high value on it. So I love that tofu can be so versatile and yet deliver the benefits I need for a healthy life. You can eat it plain, deep-fried, stir-fried, steamed, grilled or stewed. You can use it to make sauces, dressings and desserts. You can change the shape of it—slice it, dice it, grate it, purée it, crumb it—there are so many choices.

Tofu and other soy products have been widely used in Asian cuisine for more than a thousand years and yet they can be used in any type of cuisine—European, Middle Eastern and South American—as you will discover in this book.

In 2007, I started Healthy Soy Cooking to help inspire healthy living and to teach innovative ways to cook with tofu and other soy products such as edamame, miso, soy sauce, soymilk and more.

Since then I have been creating various soy dishes; and not just for Japanese styles, but also for other cuisines I learnt through my commercial cooking days, working in various restaurants. This is the book where I can finally share with you the recipes that I have been teaching and creating for almost 20 years.

So here's hoping I can inspire you to eat and live healthily, and open up your world to the magic of these healthy and tasty soy dishes!

Soy story—go natural!

Firstly, not all the soybeans are the same.

It is important for you to know that while soy is very healthy when it is in its natural form, there is a version of soy out there that research shows may not be as healthy for us, and that is soy that has been genetically modified (GMO) and highly processed, such as soy protein isolate (SPI) or texturised vegetable protein (TVP), which are normally made of GMO soy beans.

My recommendation is to choose organic or No GMO (No Genetically Modified) soybeans and soy products.

You have probably heard controversies in the media regarding soy. The soy at the centre of these discussions mostly relates to GMO soy, supplements or processed food that contains highly processed soy. Unfortunately the soybean is one of the most popular genetically modified crop and highly processed food in the world.

I believe that as long as soybeans or soy products are in a natural form, and preferably organic, they will serve your health in a very positive way. As with everything, just remember that moderation is better and that no food will be healthy in the long run if you eat it to excess over a sustained period of time.

Soybeans are packed full with fabulous nutrients and have been consumed for centuries in Japan and other Asian countries and more recently in the Western diet.

Look for the 'NO GMO' sign—if a product doesn't say this on the packet, be aware that it could potentially be GMO. Also, remember that a lot of processed food, that has nothing to do with soy—like baked goods, convenience food and processed meat—contains highly processed soy.

I am not a doctor and soy research is constantly evolving. This information comes from my studies as a soy lover and health enthusiast. Use this as an entry point for further research of your own, depending on what your particular soy concerns are.

Cooking soy with non-animal products

Tofu and soy products are fantastic to cook with meat or fish but I took the challenge to make this book plant-based, as I am on the path to a vegetarian/vegan diet.

For me, giving up meat and fish is like losing an arm but now I am more aware of animals, health and the environment. So here is the plant-based *Cooking with Soy* book!

The recipes in this book are for everyone, vegetarian/vegan or not. Cooking with tofu and without animal products is really tasty and refreshing when done right. I often hear people say 'I don't know what to do with tofu except stir fry' or 'tofu tastes so bland and boring'. I meet lots of people who are 'tofu-haters', as well as people who love tofu and want to share that love with friends and family. I would love those tofu sceptics to use this book. Trust me, I have seen many non-vegetarian people who never used tofu before, not to mention soy products, be amazed and fall in love with tasty tofu and soy meals at my cooking classes. It's a great transformation to see. This book is useful if you:

❧ would like to eat well and be healthy

❧ would like to increase your plant-based diet

❧ are thinking about becoming vegetarian

❧ are lactose intolerant

❧ have a wheat intolerance

❧ are allergic to eggs

❧ have no clue what to do with tofu

❧ hate tofu! Or know a tofu hater

❧ are a tofu lover like me

Not just traditional Japanese cuisine

There are quite a few Japanese dishes in this book because of my background, but even the Japanese recipes aren't all traditional.

The Japanese dishes you see in other countries are only one aspect of Japanese eating culture. Dishes such as teriyaki chicken, sushi and tempura are not always as healthy as many people think. They often contain a lot of refined sugar, salt and oil. In the old days, when sugar was not refined, it was okay as there were no desserts after the meal. But these days, most restaurants use refined sugar, salt and oil. So having a bento box with tempura and teriyaki in a Japanese restaurant with ice cream for dessert might not make you healthy or lose weight.

Having said all this, it is very true that Japanese cuisine is healthy; the secret is that we don't just eat what is often served up in Japanese restaurants in other countries. At home, Japanese people eat lots of alkaline food including soy. For example, we eat various types of seaweed, which is highly alkaline. Seaweed is rich in minerals yet has almost zero calories. We also eat fermented soy products, such as miso, natto and soy sauce, which are even better than other soy products. Japanese people also eat smaller portions of many dishes and do not necessarily eat a lot of desserts.

A typical afternoon or morning tea treat would be some dumplings with red beans or soybean powder, with no oil and maybe a small amount of sugar, served in a small portion. This is unlike many Western-style desserts that are full of dairy, white sugar and white flour. Thankfully our culture of desserts in the West is changing now, but it has been unhealthy for quite a while.

In the Japanese recipes in this book, I have reduced the sugar. I have also cut down the amount of oil or used oven methods instead of deep-frying. When sugar is used, I suggest it be unrefined sugar or unrefined natural sweeteners such as agave syrup, which are normally not used in Japanese cuisine wherever a sweet taste was required.

In my cooking I also use cold-pressed oil and sea salt. I do list some vegetables that would not appear in a traditional Japanese dish, because these vegetables are more widely available outside of Japan and contribute beautifully to a real fusion of cultures.

How to read recipes

All recipes are either vegan or have vegan cooking options. For me, having a food restriction is a challenge. Even though I am not vegan, I really admire vegan people giving up all animal products, and I also feel strong compassion for those who can't eat certain foods because of allergy or disease.

Those who are vegan, lactose intolerant or who have egg allergies can enjoy all the recipes in this book, and 95 per cent of the recipes are either gluten-free or have a gluten-free option. You will find the following options in the book:

V opt	— vegetarian but has a vegan cooking option
V	— vegan
GF opt	— not gluten-free but has a gluten-free cooking option
GF	— gluten-free

And for vegetarian and non-vegetarian people who might still want to use dairy products and eggs, there are vegetarian suggestions for vegan recipes, to give you a wider range of options. I want this book to be accessible to everybody, so even though I prefer to avoid dairy products when cooking, I still give recipe options with dairy for those who prefer that.

Many of the ingredients used in this book are listed in the glossary, to give you brief explanations of particular food or products you may not have encountered before.

Ingredients—healthy choice

I highly recommend using the unrefined forms of sugar, oil and salt—all ingredients we use on a daily basis. It is critical to know that the refined forms of these ingredients don't have quality nutrients. This is especially the case for many processed oils in plastic bottles that are normally sold in supermarkets, as they contain trans fat, which is harmful to the body.

But I don't want you to feel that cooking from this book is too much hassle! So please use what you're comfortable with and adjust to suit yourself. I understand that everybody is on a different eating journey so please choose ingredients that suit you the best right now, and be mindful about how you can plan and adjust for the future.

My message here is that if you could slowly use a couple of extra dollars to put better quality ingredients in your body and actually give yourself more nutrition, then it will pay off and you will save a lot more in the longer term. It is a fabulous investment for yourself and your family and will enhance how you feel about yourself. Many people start to watch what they eat when they get sick; so consider preventing unnecessary sickness by treating your body and mind with care, instead of being forced to look for a cure later on.

Over the last 10 years, I have made small changes—such as changing first the salt I use, then sugar, then cooking oils—which have transformed and improved my diet, while maintaining the taste. You are what you eat and I really believe that everybody deserves good health. This book will help you to achieve it.

Grating

In my recipes, I use the term 'finely grated' when I want the ingredient to be grated using a Japanese-style grater, a special type of grater that grates to a fine mush. In the photo below, you can see a Western-style grater and the end product—food grated in a long shape. The Japanese grater on the right, which is mainly used for condiments like ginger and daikon (radish) in Japan, grates very finely.

So that you know which grater I have used, I have used the word 'grate' for the long-shaped grater, and 'finely grated' for the very fine grating. For 'finely grated', use a Japanese grater (available from an Asian grocery or $2 shop), a microplane or the finest side of the stainless steel grater.

Soy family

Always check that the label on any purchased soy products has a 'NO GMO' sign, meaning 'no genetically modified organisims'.

Aburaage

Aburaage is a thin, deep-fried tofu. The tofu is sliced, the water is drained away, and then it is deep-fried until the outside becomes crisp and golden brown but the inside remains white. It has a sponge-like texture and soaks up liquid like a sponge, which means it soaks up the flavour of items it is cooked with. It is used in soups, noodle dishes and sushi (Inari Zushi). Aburaage is available frozen.

atsuage

edamame, shelled

edamame

kinako

red miso

white miso

natto

okara

soymilk

Atsuage

It is a thicker version of aburaage. Atsuage is made by deep-frying large blocks of fresh tofu. It is golden and crispy on the outside, but soft and smooth on the inside, like silken tofu. Like aburaage, it soaks up the taste of any other flavours it is cooked in. It is available fresh from the refrigeration section in Asian grocery shops.

Edamame

These are soy beans, picked green before maturity. They have a firm and crispy texture. In Japan, boiled whole pod of edamame with salt are eaten as a snack with beer, especially in summer (summer is the harvest season of edamame). Edamame is available frozen (in pods or shelled) in Asian grocery shops.

Kinako

Kinako is a powder of roasted whole soybeans. Kinako is widely used in traditional Japanese sweets, known as 'wagashi'. Most sticky rice cakes (*mochi*) or sticky rice flour dumplings (*dango*) are coated with kinako. Available in Asian grocery shops.

Miso

Miso is fermented soybean paste. It is most often made by double fermentation process from a combination of soybeans, koji (cultured grain) and sea salt. Koji can be made of rice, barley or soybeans. Names for miso such as rice miso, barley miso and bean miso are culture specific. There are hundreds of miso in Japan but about 80% of miso are rice miso. Many think all miso is gluten free but barley miso isn't gluten free.

MISO TYPES CATEGORISED BY KOJI (CULTURED GRAIN)
- Rice miso (most common)
- Barley miso (contains gluten)
- Bean miso (100 per cent soy beans)

Miso is typically salty, but its flavour and aroma depends on various factors including the ingredients and fermentation process. Different varieties of miso have been described as salty, sweet, earthy, fruity and savoury, and there is an extremely wide range of miso available. The taste, aroma, texture and appearance of any specific miso vary by miso type as well as the region and season the miso was made for. The ingredients used, temperature and duration of fermentation, salt content, variety of koji, and fermenting vessel all contribute.

THE MOST COMMON FLAVOUR/COLOUR CATEGORIES OF MISO

❧ Shiro miso—white miso, yellowish colour. Sweet, mild, low in sodium.

❧ Aka miso—red miso, dark reddish brown color. Salty and strong flavour.

❧ Awase miso—mixed miso, blend of red and white miso, Medium flavour.

Available in some supermarkets and Asian grocers, refrigerated or not refrigerated.

Natto

Natto is made by adding beneficial bacteria (*Bacillus natto*) to fermented, steamed whole soybeans and has been recognised as one of Japan's most unique traditional health foods. Fermentation enhances the nutrition of soybeans and develops a unique smell, flavour and texture. Natto has a very strong smell, akin to strong cheese and has a nutty flavour. Stirring the natto produces lots of spiderweb-like strings. In Japan, natto is most commonly eaten at breakfast to accompany rice.

Natto has recently received keen attention because of its natural enzyme, *Nattokinase* that has health benefits, especially known for anti-blood clotting capacities.

It is available frozen in Asian grocery shops.

Okara

Okara is the ivory pulp that is left over after the soymilk is squeezed from soybeans. It's moist and crumbly and as flavourful as a wad of paper towels. Traditionally, we cook okara with stock, soy sauce, mirin and some vegetables, which is not quite tasty from my point of view. Recently in Japan, okara is being used in baked sweets as okara is much more filling and has a better nutritional value than flour. That is why okara sweets have been a huge hit in the diet industry in Japan. Okara is low in fat, high in fibre, and also contains protein, calcium, iron and riboflavin and has only 94 calories per cup.

Soymilk

Soymilk is a rich, creamy liquid obtained by soaking and grinding whole soybeans and straining or hydrating whole, full-fat soy flour. Soymilk may have a strong bean taste; however, the intensity of flavour is directly influenced by the method of preparation. There are three basic methods.

1. Chinese-style traditional soymilk method (full bean flavour): Soaked soybeans are ground with cold water

2. Japanese-style good-tasting soymilk method (less bean flavour): Soaked soybeans are ground with hot water.

3. Western-style good-tasting soymilk method (a touch of bean flavour): Dry soybeans are dehulled and put into enzyme inactivator to inactivate enzyme with hot water.

Non-processed (Chinese-style) fresh soymilk is an everyday regular drink as dairy milk is in the West. It is popular not only in China but also Hong Kong, Singapore, Malaysia, Thailand and Taiwan. Because of the strong full bean flavour, this style is not popular in other countries.It is available from the refrigerated section of the Asian grocer.

Japanese-style soymilk is quite close to the Chinese style. The flavoured variety is also quite popular in Japan. Plain flavours are available in Australia but only in a few Japanese grocery shops.

Western-style soymilk is the most popular in Western countries, and is even popular in Japan. Available in aseptic tetra brick or retort standing pouches, it can be sold without refrigeration. Various types (of regular, low-fat and non-fat soymilk) are available, as well as flavoured varieties, such as vanilla, chocolate and more. Refined sugar and oil are often added to the soymilk, including plain, to make the soymilk sweeter or give a creamy, rich texture. Please read the label and choose a quality soymilk that doesn't contain refined sugar or oil.

Soy sauce

Soy sauce is an essential condiment and ingredient in many Asian countries. Soy sauce is a naturally brewed salty, brown liquid made from fermented soybeans mixed with water, wheat and salt.

The process for producing soy sauce requires a mixture of soybeans, salt and water left to ferment. After the fermentation period, the mixture is ground, boiled and filtered. The resulting liquid is soy sauce

The fermentation period varies from brand to brand and country to country. The average Japanese soy sauce's fermentation period is for six months, the longest is three years.

Unfortunately some brands use additives for convenience or add fermentation accelerant to speed up the fermentation period. Even worse, some 'soy sauce' are made synthetically from hydrolysed plant protein blended with caramel colouring and corn syrup.

Light-colored (higher sodium than ordinary say sauce) soy sauce (*usukichi syoyu*) and light soy sauce, and low-sodium soy sauce as well as dark soy sauce that is less salty, sweeter, thicker and darker than light soy sauce are also available.

Soy sauce is available in supermarkets and Asian groceries.

Tamari

A type of soy sauce that's made with less or no wheat, tamari is suitable for those with wheat allergies.

Tamari is darker in appearance and richer in flavour than soy sauce. It is said to be the original type of Japanese soy sauce, as its recipe is closest to the soy sauce originally introduced to Japan from China. Tamari comes from the word *tamaru* in Japanese, which means 'collect, gather or accumulate'. Tamari was originally a liquid by-product of miso, obtained at the end of its process.

Tofu

Said to have originated in China, about 2000 years ago, tofu is made by curdling soymilk with coagulant. The most widely used coagulant is *nigari*, the Japanese word for magnesium chloride. Japanese tofu is traditionally made with nigari. Another coagulent is calcium sulfate, which is to produce Chinese-style tofu.

There are many different types of tofu. See Types of Tofu.

Tofu puffs

These are golden squares of bean curd that have been deep-fried. It has been deep-fried more than aburaage or atsuage so the outside is chewier and harder. Unlike atsuage, tofu puffs have a hollow centre. Like other deep-fried tofu, tofu puffs are super absorbent. They are not used in Japan. They are used in Chinese, Malay, Singaporean, Taiwanese, Thai and Vietnamese cuisine.

Available in cellophane bags in the refrigeration section of Asian grocery shops, they are sold under a variety of names, such as Bean Kow or Bean Curd Puffs or Tofu Puffs.

Tofu skins

Also called bean curd skin or bean curd (tofu) sheet. Tofu skins are known as yuba in Japanese.

They are made by lifting the skin that forms on top of boiling soymilk. The skins are collected and dried into yellowish sheets or rolled sticks. Fresh tofu skins can be purchased as well; fresh tofu skins are popular and considered a delicacy in Japan.

Dried skins need to be reconstituted in water before use. Sheets are used as wrappers for food, which may be deep-fried, steamed or simmered and the sticks can be simmered or added to soup.

They are available as dried tofu skin in Asian grocery shops.

Tempeh

Tempeh is fermented cooked soybeans with a *Rhizopus* moulds (tempeh starter). This natural culturing and controlled fermentation process binds the soybeans into a compact white cake form. Tempeh is originally from Indonesia and has been a staple source of protein for several hundred years. It is now rapidly becoming popular all over the world as people are aware of its health benefits.

Tempeh has a firm texture and a nutty flavour. It is very versatile and can be used in recipes in different ways. Normally tempeh is sliced or cut in cubes and fried until the surface is crisp and golden brown. Tempeh can be used as an ingredient in soups, spreads, salads and sandwiches. Tempeh, both plain and marinated varieties, are now commonly available in many supermarkets as well as in Asian shops and health food stores.

aburaage

tofu puffs

silken tofu

firm tofu

tofu skins

tempeh

tofu, tubed

Types of tofu

Even though tofu is a really popular food in Japan, there are more varieties of tofu available outside of Japan. In Japan, the basic types of tofu are soft (silken) and firm (momen) but elsewhere, there are three types of tofu, categorised by texture—soft, firm and hard.

Soft

SILKEN TOFU

Kinugoshi-dofu in Japanese, means literally 'silken tofu' because of its fine and smooth texture.

This is the softest tofu. It is sold in the cold section of the supermarket in a plastic tub soaking in water or on the supermarket shelves in a tetra pack.

It has a smooth and silky texture with a creamy flavour because it is made with denser, richer soymilk.

It is solidified in the container unlike other types of tofu and therefore contains the highest moisture content of all fresh tofu, giving it a delicate consistency.

There are different kinds of silken tofu, some which are slightly firmer. They can be described as silken firm, pressed silken, original or classic, it depends on brands. I like these the best as they don't contain as much as water, which means it is easier to cook, yet it still has a smooth texture.

Soft tofu is ideal for:

❀ Eat as it is—add to salad or soup
❀ Purée—for lightly textured dip or as the base of sauces, dressings or desserts
❀ Dry-fry—to produce a scrambled, egg-like texture
❀ Deep-fry—only silken firm tofu or other firmer version of silken tofu

Medium

FIRM TOFU

Momen-dofu in Japanese, literally means 'cotton tofu' because of the process of moulding tofu in cotton-lined fabric.

Firm tofu is mostly sold in a plastic tub with water. You can also find it vacuum-packed.

It has been separated from whey and the curdled soy first, then drained and pressed to remove water. This type of tofu is dense and solid but still contains a great amount of moisture. It has the firmness of raw meat but bounces back readily when pressed. Firm tofu is ideal for:

❀ Stir-frying, grilling, deep-frying
❀ Adding to soups
❀ Puréeing for denser textured dip, sauce or dressing base and desserts

🦪 Marinating

🦪 Using as mince meat substitute when crumbled

Hard

HARD TOFU OR EXTRA FIRM TOFU

This is the kind found in plastic and is almost always vacuum-packed. You will find it labelled as 'hard tofu' or 'extra firm'. This tofu is like a brick as it is very dense and solid, with a meaty texture. It has the firmness of cooked meat.

I have found that Asian brands of tofu, sold in Asian groceries, are usually harder and more tightly packed than ones found in your local supermarket. You can also find 'extra firm' tofu sold in a tub, which is not as hard as the vacuum-packed version.

In my opinion, this tofu is the easiest to cook with because it has the least amount of water content. The most important part of tofu cooking is getting rid of excess water, according to the dish you are preparing (please see the section on How To Get Rid of Excess Water). You will need to remove excess water from silken or firm tofu for some dishes but for this hard tofu, you don't need to do anything—you can use it straight from the package, whatever dish you are cooking.

DRY TOFU

Chinese 'dry tofu' has an even harder texture than hard tofu. Despite its name, this tofu has not been dried. It has simply had a large amount of water pressed out of it.

Dry tofu contains the least amount of water of all fresh tofu and is therefore the hardest of all fresh tofu. It has the firmness of fully cooked meat and a slight rubbery texture, a bit like paneer (Indian cheese). It is widely used as a meat substitute in China and Taiwan. Hard or dry tofu is ideal for:

🦪 Stir-frying and grilling (Dry tofu needs to be thinly sliced or shredded)

🦪 Adding shreds to salad, pasta or noodle dishes

🦪 Crumbling to use as a mince substitute

From left: soft tofu; medium tofu; hard tofu

Soft	silken tofu (sold in a tub or tetra pack)	very soft
	silken firm tofu pressed silken tofu classic or original tofu (sold in a tub)	soft
Medium	firm tofu (mostly sold in a tub) extra firm tofu (in a tub)	firm
Hard	extra firm tofu (sold in vacuum packs) hard tofu (sold in vacuum packs)	hard
	hard tofu (Asian brand) (sold in vacuum packs)	harder
	Chinese dry tofu	hardest

*Labels and textures of tofu varieties vary from brand to brand and country to country.

How to remove excess water from tofu

Almost 90 per cent of tofu is water. Successful tofu cooking is all about removing any excess water from the tofu.

We can remove a little or a lot of water, it depends on what sort of dish you are cooking. For example, for salads, you don't want to remove too much water; whereas when you are making dips or deep-fried dishes, you will need to remove the water more thoroughly. Otherwise, the water will come to the surface of your dips, or splash the oil when you fry.

Following are some examples of methods for removing water. In Japan, many people use the microwave for convenience and this does do a good job, but I don't suggest it here for health reasons.

REMOVE WATER LIGHTLY

- Pat the tofu with kitchen paper.
- Place tofu on a tilted chopping board. Let it stand for 10 minutes.
- Place tofu on a plate or strainer and let stand for another 10 minutes.

REMOVE WATER MODERATELY

- Wrap tofu in cheesecloth or paper towels and place on a tilted chopping board for 30 minutes
- Place a light weight on top and let stand for 30 minutes.

REMOVE WATER THOROUGHLY

- Put the tofu in a pot of boiling water and boil for 5 minutes. Drain if you want to keep the shape.
- Break the tofu and boil it for 2 minutes and drain if you don't need to keep the shape.
- Place a heavy weight on top and let it stand for 1 hour or more—it depends on the type of tofu you are using. The weight has to be not too heavy to break the tofu. The softer the tofu, the lighter the weight.

HOW TO STORE LEFTOVER TOFU

Tofu doesn't last long once opened. Place the leftover tofu into a container or small bowl, covered with water. Put the lid on or cover it with plastic wrap then refrigerate. Use the leftover tofu within one week and change the water daily.

TIP FOR EATING FRESH TOFU

When you open the packet, the surface of tofu is sometimes slightly slimy. Place tofu in a bowl and cover with water. Rub the tofu gently. Then replace with clean water, preferably filtered, enough to cover the tofu and leave for 5 to 10 minutes.

boil tofu

wash with water

flatten with rolling pin

open up pouch

How to handle deep-fried tofu

HOW TO *ABURANUKI*

When cooking with deep-fried tofu such as aburaage, atsuage and tofu puff, you will need to get rid of the excess oil on the surface. This process is called *aburanuki* in Japanese.

By doing this, the tofu will absorb the seasoning better and also be able to remove unwanted smells from old oil or any freezer smell (aburaage are sold frozen).

There are two ways to get rid of oil:

❧ You can simply pour boiling water on deep-fried tofu on all sides and wash with water. Pat dry.

❧ You can boil deep-fried tofu for 2 to 5 minutes. Rinse with water and pat dry.

Both ways work the same, just choose a method depending on what type of dish you are making.

If your deep-fried tofu is for grilling or oven baking, like in the Aburaage Samosa, Aburaage and Chia Seed Dressing, I simply pour boiling water over the tofu or boil for 2 to 3 minutes.

If your deep-fried tofu is for simmering, like in the Quinoa Inari recipe, the boiling method is better; boil for at least 5 minutes.

I prefer the boiling method and tend to boil longer. We don't know what sort of oil is used to deep-fry them so it is better to get rid of as much oil as you can. The boiling method makes deep-fried tofu softer and fluffier as well.

How to make pouches easily

Making pouches can be difficult. Here is the tip to open them easily.

1. Get rid of oil first using a method described above.
2. Place the aburaage on a cutting board and flatten it with a rolling pin. Traditionally, in Japan this is done with long chopsticks used especially for cooking. Please make sure you use a round chopstick not a square chopstick! This makes it easier to open the the aburaage as a pouch.
3. Cut the aburaage in half.
4. Open up the aburaage from cut side to make pouches.

Homemade tofu

I really love freshly made tofu. It tastes nothing like store-bought packet tofu. While it does take time to make, it is well worth the effort.

You need:
Blender or food processor
Tofu cloth (or muslin cheesecloth)
Large pot
Ladle
Slotted spoon
Bowl
Strainer
Cooking thermometer

Tofu mould
2 cups soybeans
9g nigari flake*
100ml (3½fl oz) water
* if you purchase nigari water, use 100ml
   (3½fl oz) nigari water

1. Wash the soybeans well then soak them in three times the amount of water overnight (6 cups). Soaking time varies with seasons; in summer, about 8 hours, spring and autumn it's 15 hours and in winter, 20 hours.

2. Put about half of the soybeans in a blender and add enough water (from the soaking water) to cover the beans. Blend for about 2 to 3 minutes until the beans are very finely ground.

3. You may need to add more water and blend further. Do the same with the remaining half of the soybeans.

4. Pour the bean mixture into a very large pot and add 5 cups of water then cook over a high heat, stirring constantly. Make sure you scrape the bottom since the fine soy pulp tends to get burnt on the bottom of the pot. Skim off any foam left on top.

5. Meanwhile, dissolve the nigari in 100ml (3½fl oz) water.

6. Preparation step—line a strainer with cheesecloth for later.

7. When boiled, it will foam up and rise to the rim of the pot. If you are late turning down the heat, it will boil over so to keep an eye on the mixture as it gets hotter, and as soon as the mixture begins to rise, reduce the heat.

8. Once it has been brought to the boil, reduce the heat to low and cook for a further 10 minutes. Stir consistently from the bottom.

9. Strain the hot mixture through a colander lined with cheesecloth that is sitting over a

1.

2.

tofu moulds

make a mould

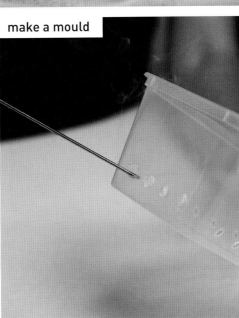

3.

bowl or pot. Squeeze out the liquid by carefully gathering up the sides of your cloth and twisting it closed. The liquid is soymilk.

10. Use a very sturdy spatula to press down on the bag to extract as much of the liquid as possible.

11. The pulp left in the cloth is called okara (see the okara recipes in this book).

12. Quickly rinse out the cooking pot and put it back on the stove. Transfer the soymilk to the pot, and cook it over a medium heat until the soymilk reaches between 70 to 75°C (160–165°F). Remove the pot from the heat.

13. In a whirlpool pattern, add half of the nigari water to the soymilk by using a spatula. Stirring slowly, which is more like pushing down the nigari to the bottom, add the remaining nigari water in the same way. This time, stir on the surface only, as if drawing a cross, a few times. You'll notice that the soymilk is beginning to coagulate; cover the pot and let it sit until the water is completely clear (see picture). This usually takes 30–45 minutes.

14. In the meantime, prepare your mould by lining it with clean, wet cheesecloths that have been wrung out.

15. Spoon the coagulated soy from the pot by using the slotted spoon (with holes). Keep filling the mould with this coagulated soy; you may need to wait for some of the liquid to drain out a bit before adding more. Once you've added all the curd, fold the cloth over to cover.

16. Put some kind of weight on top, to help press out the liquid. If you like soft tofu, simply let it stand without any weight.

17. Let is stand for 8 minutes or more to allow extra liquid to drain.

18. The longer you leave it, and the heavier the weight, the firmer the tofu will become.

19. Serve with grated ginger, chopped ginger and soy sauce.

Tip: You can still make this without a mould. Simply leave the tofu curd in a lined strainer.

You can purchase tofu moulds online but you can also make the mould with a plastic take-away container.

Heat the metal barbeque skewer and make several holes on the side and bottom of the plastic container; the holes drain out the water.

You can purchase special tofu cloth, but you can also use cheesecloth (muslin).

9a.   9b.   9c.

10.   11.   13a.

13b.   15.   16.

APPETISERS

Tofu Dips

These colourful dips are perfect for a party. Ingredients such as tofu, avocado and olives make dips rich and creamy—most people can't even tell they are made from tofu. Enjoy with your favourite crackers or fresh vegetable sticks.

Avocado and Lime Dip

75g (2½oz) firm or silken firm tofu
150g (5oz) avocado flesh (without skin)
1 tablespoon lime juice
1 teaspoon sea salt

1.   Remove excess water from tofu by boiling or let stand with weight for 1 hour.

2.   Place all ingredients, except tofu, into a small food processor and process until smooth. Add tofu and process further.

Olive and Caper Dip

150g (5oz) firm or silken firm tofu
5 pitted black olives (130g/4½oz)
2 teaspoons capers
1 tablespoon parsley, chopped

1.   Remove excess water from tofu by boiling or let stand with weight for 1 hour.

2.   Place olives, capers and parsley in a small food processor and process until smooth. Add the tofu and process further.

Sundried Tomato Dip

150g (5oz) firm or silken firm tofu
100g (3½oz) marinated sundried tomato, chopped
70g (2½oz) marinated red pepper, chopped roughly
2 tablespoons marinated oil from sundried tomato jar

1.   Remove excess water from tofu by boiling or let stand with weight for 1 hour.

2.   Place sundried tomato, red pepper and marinade oil in a small food processor and process well. Add tofu and process until smooth.

Tip: The key to blending well is to firstly process the chunky ingredients very well, and then add the tofu or softer ingredients such as avocado.

Soy Hummus

Hummus is a very popular Middle Eastern dip made from chickpeas. Why don't you try it with soy? It's as good as chickpea hummus.

250g (9oz) soybeans (or cooked 500g/17½oz) soybeans)
50ml (1¾fl oz) extra virgin olive oil
1½ teaspoons sea salt
3 tablespoons tahini
2 tablespoons lemon juice
1 teaspoon cumin powder
3 tablespoons water
Pinch of paprika
Extra olive oil for serving

1. Soak the soybeans overnight.

2. Cook the soybeans within a pressure cooker for 15 minutes or boil until cooked.

3. Drain the soybeans.

4. Place the soybeans and the rest of the ingredients and process until smooth. You may want to add extra water for a softer texture.

5. Transfer the hummus into a bowl and sprinkle a pinch of paprika over it.

6. Serve with your favourite bread or fresh vegetable sticks.

Soy and Mushroom Pâté

This pâté is my favourite. Adding just a touch of porcini mushroom gives it a deeper flavour. It is perfect for a picnic or to simply enjoy with your favourite bread and a glass of wine.

250g (9oz) mushrooms, sliced
1 tablespoon dried porcini mushroom
2 tablespoons olive oil
1 clove garlic, finely chopped
½ teaspoon sea salt
1 cup cooked soybeans
½ teaspoon tamari
½ teaspoon lemon juice

1. Soak the porcini with 1 tablespoon water. Keep the water.

2. Chop the porcini and set it aside.

3. Heat the frying pan over a low heat and add 1 tablespoon of oil and garlic.

4. Sauté the garlic slowly to infuse the flavour and aroma then add mushroom, porcini and ¼ teaspoon sea salt, and sauté over a medium heat until mushroom turns soft.

5. Add the porcini water and cook further until water is almost gone.

6. Place the mushroom, soybeans, ¼ teaspoon of salt, tamari, lemon juice and 1 tablespoon oil in a blender and blend until smooth.

7. Serve with your favourite bread.

Edamame Spread

I love this simple taste; sometimes I add black pepper or curry powder to make it different. If you add a little more water to it, you can also serve it as a dip.

200g (7oz) shelled frozen edamame
    (500g/17½oz with shell)
2 tablespoons extra virgin olive oil
½ teaspoon lemon juice
½ teaspoon sea salt

1.   Boil the edamame until soft.

2.   Place all the ingredients in a food processor and process until smooth. If the texture is too hard, you can add 1 tablespoon soymilk or water.

3.   Serve with toasted bread or gluten-free bread.

Tip: You can add your favourite flavour, such as black pepper, curry powder or cumin powder.

Agedashi Dofu

Deep-fried tofu with broth

This traditional tofu dish is everybody's favourite tofu dish. Just follow the two tips below and you will make it beautifully and safely!

300g (10½oz) x 1 packet /block firm or silken firm tofu
Potato starch for dusting
Neutral oil for deep-frying

Broth
150ml (5fl oz) water
1 teaspoon instant konbu dashi powder
1 tablespoon mirin
1 tablespoon soy sauce

Garnish
2 tablespoons finely grated daikon
2 tablespoons chopped green onions (scallions)
1 tablespoon finely grated fresh ginger

1. Remove the tofu from the packet, place on a plate and cover with paper towel. Allow to stand for 30 minutes and drain off any excess liquid.

2. To make broth, combine 150ml (5fl oz) water and the konbu dashi powder in a small saucepan and bring to the boil. Add mirin and boil a little. Reduce the heat, add the soy sauce and return to the boil and then turn off the heat.

3. Slice the tofu in half to make two squares. Then slice each square in half again to make a total of 4 equal portions.

4.   Carefully pat dry each portion of tofu with paper towel to remove the excess moisture.

5.   Dust the surfaces of the tofu with the potato starch and gently shake the tofu to remove any excess. (For best results coat the tofu just prior to cooking.)Heat 1cm to 2cm (½–¾in) of oil in a frying pan over medium heat (around 170°C/340°F). Add the tofu and fry for about 4 minutes on each side or until slightly golden. Drain well on absorbent paper.

6.   To serve, place tofu portions into small individual serving bowls, pour over the broth and top the tofu with the daikon, shallots and ginger.

Gluten-free option: Use tamari instead of soy sauce.

Tips: Instead of soy sauce, use *usukuchi syoyu*, which is a light soy sauce.

Dust the tofu with potato flour just before frying—make sure your oil is hot enough (when you leave tofu covered with flour too long, the water in the tofu comes out and makes it soggy).

Once you put the tofu in oil, please do not touch if for at least 3 minutes. If you touch tofu while cooking, you might break the tofu and then water could come out, causing the oil to splash.

Agedashi Dofu

Edamame Tofu

Edamame Tofu

It is wonderful to have colourful tofu. Edamame gives it a beautiful green colour. Not only is it visually appealing, but kuzu, the super healthy thickener, actually adds even more nutritional value. It is fantastic to eat either cold or warm, and you can also eat it with a tomato sauce like you would with gnocchi.

100g (3½oz) shelled frozen edamame
1 cup vegetable stock or kelp stock (or 1 cup water, 1 teaspoon vegetable stock powder or kelp stock powder, pinch of salt; boil well)
¼ teaspoon sea salt
60g (2oz) kuzu
100g (3½oz) silken tofu

Broth
150ml (5fl oz) water
1 teaspoon instant konbu dashi powder
1 tablespoon mirin
1 tablespoon soy sauce

Garnish
Shallot, julienned and soak in cold water
Ginger, julienned and soak in cold water

1. To make broth, combine 150ml (5fl oz) water and the konbu dashi powder in a small saucepan and bring to the boil. Then add mirin and boil a little. Reduce the heat, add the soy sauce and return to the boil and turn off the heat. Refrigerate until cooled down.

2. Boil the edamame in a saucepan or simply pour boiling water over them.

3. Place the edamame and stock in a blender or food processor and blend well.

4. Add salt, kuzu and break the tofu by hand into the blender. Blend until smooth.

5.   Pour the mixture into a saucepan and cook over medium heat. Stir consistently and cook until very thick.

6.   Place the plastic wrap onto four individual bowls or ramekins. Plastic wrap has to be big enough to make a ball.

7.   Pour the mixture into the wrap then twist and close on the top to make a ball.

8.   Put the tofu in a fridge or, if you are in a hurry, you can cool with ice.

9.   Serve with cold broth and garnish with julienned ginger and shallot.

Gluten-free option: Use tamari instead of soy sauce.

Serving suggestions: This dish is also delicious when warm. Serve with wasabi and soy sauce

You can also use it to replace gnocchi in other recipes. To make gnocchi shapes, scoop the mixture with a spoon and shape with another spoon to make the gnocchi shape; then put into ice water. Serve with freshly made tomato sauce (see the recipe for Tofu Lasagna).

Easy Aburaage Samosa

Instead of pastry, use aburaage and just bake it in the oven instead of deep-frying it. This makes a much easier and healthier samosa. People who have tried it have also told me that the aburaage makes the samosas much tastier.

½ cup frozen peas
4 sheets aburaage (refer to 'How to handle deep-fried tofu')
2 teaspoons neutral oil
½ onion (about 90g/3oz), chopped
2 teaspoons curry powder
2 large potatoes (about 600g/21oz)
1 teaspoon sea salt
4 tablespoons egg-free soy mayonnaise

1.   Preheat the oven to 200°C (400°F).

2.   Pour boiling water over frozen peas. Set aside.

3.   Boil the aburaage in water for 1 or 2 minutes to get rid of excess oil from the aburaage. This will not only remove oil but also any unwanted smell from old oil and let the seasoning soak better.

4.   Drain and cool the aburaage with water.

5.   Place the aburaage on a cutting board and flatten it with a rolling pin. This makes it easier to open the aburaage as a pouch.

6.   Cut the aburaage in half.

7.   Carefully open up the aburaage from the cut side to make pouches, then turn pouches inside out. Set aside.

8.   Place the oil and onion in a small frying pan and fry until slightly transparent; add curry powder and cook for 2 minutes then add frozen peas and cook for 2 minutes. Set aside.

9.   Boil the potato with a pinch of salt (extra). Mash the potato, add the salt, mayonnaise, fried onion mixture and mix well.

10. Divide the potato mixture into 8 portions. Place the mixture into a pocket and shape into a triangle.

11. Bake in the oven for 10 minutes.

Tip: Serve with raita or chutney. For a vegetarian option, you can use whole egg mayonnaise or Japanese mayonnaise.

Garlic Butter Edamame

This recipe literally takes 5 minutes or less to make. You can cook it in a frying pan or in the oven if you are using the oven for another dish.

200g (7oz) frozen edamame
1 tablespoon non-hydrogenated non-dairy butter
1 teaspoon garlic flakes
1½ teaspoon sea salt

1. Pour boiling water onto edamame and drain.

2. Place the butter and garlic flakes in a frying pan and heat over medium heat; sauté for 1 minute.

3. Add the edamame and toss to combine.

4. Serve immediately.

5. Alternatively, preheat the oven to 200°C (400°F).

6. Line the baking tray with baking sheet.

7. Place the edamame, butter and garlic together and mix well then bake for 10 minutes.

Tip: For vegetarians, use butter instead of non-dairy butter. You can also use fresh finely chopped garlic. If using a pan, make sure to infuse the garlic flavour into the butter by sautéing for an extra 2 minutes at a medium-low heat. Using an oven, bake for an extra 5 minutes.

Wasabi Edamame

This is a really easy edamame dish. If you love wasabi, you will love this.

200g (7oz) frozen edamame
15g (½oz) wasabi powder
3 teaspoons sea salt

1. Pour boiling water over frozen edamame and leave for 5 seconds or just blanch.

2. Place the edamame, wasabi and salt in a plastic bag and shake well.

Tip: You can also just put frozen edamame and the rest of the ingredients in a bag and let it all stand until defrosted.

Serves 4 as appetiser/2 as entrée

Japanese-style Edamame Vichyssoise

This is a very simple soup to make and yet it is very tasty. I love adding some basil and lemon to make it special. You can also enjoy it as a warm soup.

1½ cup boiling water
1½ teaspoon konbu and mushroom dashi powder
¼ teaspoon sea salt
200g (7oz) shelled frozen edamame
frozen edamame, for garnish

1.   Place the boiling water and dashi powder in a pot and boil for 2 minutes. Set aside.

2.   Boil the water and add a pinch of salt, then place the edamame in the water and cook until the edamame float to the surface. Drain and set aside (keep some for garnish).

3. Place the cooked edamame, dashi and salt in a blender and blend well. Pour into a bowl and place it in a fridge.

Tip: You can also use vegetable stock powder instead of Japanese dashi powder.

Grilled Rice Paper Roll with Millet and Tofu

I love using grains, such as millet, as a filling for rice paper rolls. It makes a rice paper roll become a substantial entrée. I also enjoy eating the filling on its own. It is like having light fried rice, even though it isn't fried.

1½ teaspoons dried shiitake mushrooms*, soaked in 1 cup water (keep the water for cooking)
½ cup millet, washed
1 teaspoon sea salt
150g (5oz) firm tofu
60g (2oz) snow peas, julienned
25g (¾oz) pickled ginger, julienned
8 x rice paper sheets
2 teaspoons neutral oil for frying

Dipping sauce ingredients

Creamy sesame sauce
1 tablespoon hulled tahini
1 tablespoon miso
1 tablespoon rice vinegar
1 tablespoon water

Soy vinegar
1 tablespoon soy sauce
2 tablespoons rice vinegar

Gluten free option: For a gluten-free option, use tamari instead of soy sauce. Substitute barley miso for rice miso, as barley contains wheat.

1. Slice the shiitake mushroom (keep all the soaking water for cooking).

2. To cook millet, place the millet, sliced mushroom, salt and 1 cup of mushrooms in soaking water (you may need to add more water to make up one cup). Mix well. Break the tofu by hand and add to the pot. Place the lid on and bring to the boil over a high heat; then reduce to a low heat and cook for 15 minutes. Turn off heat and leave for 10 minutes. Mix well.

3. Place the millet into the bowl and add snow peas and ginger and mix well.

4. Wet the rice paper with lukewarm water and place the millet and begin to roll (see rice paper rolling images for Fresh Rice Paper Rolls).

5. Heat the frying pan with oil over a medium heat and place in the rolls, one by one.

6. Cook until golden, then turn and cook on other side.

7. To make the dipping sauces, mix each set of ingredients together. Serve with dipping sauces.

Fresh Rice Paper Roll with Chia and Thai Marinade Tofu

This is a fantastic way to enjoy tofu and chia seeds and eat lots of vegetables. It is an easy, light and healthy entrée.

200g (7oz) firm tofu
8 x rice paper sheets
1 tablespoon chia seeds, soak with 2 tablespoons water
80g (2½oz) snow peas, julienned
80g (2½oz) carrots, cut into thin strips
Half red capsicum, cut into thin strips

Thai marinade
120ml (4fl oz) sweet chilli sauce
30ml (1fl oz) lime juice
4 teaspoons soy sauce
3 teaspoons sesame oil
coriander, chopped

1. Pat the tofu with kitchen paper and cut into strips.

2. To make Thai marinade, mix all ingredients in a bowl.

3. Place the tofu into the marinade; mix and leave for at least two hours.

4. Wet the rice paper with lukewarm water.

5. Spread the chia seeds on the rice paper.

6. Place the tofu and the veggies, and roll.

7. Fold in the sides then roll up to enclose the filling. Serve with remaining marinade mix

Tip: You can also sprinkle chia seeds, without soaking them, on the rice paper. This is easier than spread-soaked chia seeds. Make sure your filling touches the chia seeds so they get lots of moisture. Leave at least 10 minutes after rolling to make sure all chia seeds absorb liquid.

Gluten-free option: Use tamari instead of soy.

Rolled Cabbage with Tofu Fish and Japanese Broth

Make a fish-like paste using tofu and potato flour and roll with Chinese cabbage. This is a very elegant Japanese dish—perfect for entertaining! For a daily meal, you can simply grill the paste to enjoy as mock fish.

2 bunches English spinach
6 pieces Chinese cabbage

Paste
300g (10½oz) firm tofu
2 tablespoons finely grated potato (see the Grating section)
2 tablespoons potato flour (starch)
½ teaspoon sea salt

Japanese thick broth
150ml (5fl oz) water
1 teaspoon MSG-free konbu dashi powder
1 tablespoon mirin
1 tablespoon soy sauce
2 teaspoons water
2 teaspoons potato starch

Garnish
1 carrot, shaped into a flower using a vegetable cutter

1. Remove excess water from tofu by boiling or let stand with weight for 30 minutes.

2. To make a fish-like paste, place the tofu, grated potato, potato flour and salt in a food processor and process until smooth.

3. To make the broth, combine 150ml (5fl oz) water with the konbu dashi powder in a small saucepan and bring to the boil, then add mirin and boil a little. Reduce the heat, add the soy sauce and return to the boil.

4. Add the potato flour to the broth, which has been mixed well beforehand, and then mix very quickly and cook until thickened.

5. To prepare the vegetables, steam or boil spinach, Chinese cabbage and carrot.

6. To roll, place down the cabbage then place tofu mixture and spinach side by side.

7. Fold over one end to make a base then roll until the end. Repeat this process with the remaining mixture.

8. Steam the roll for 15 minutes.

9. To serve, cut the roll into four pieces and pour the sauce and top with carrot.

Gluten-free Option: For a gluten-free option, use tamari instead of soy sauce.

Tip: You can use light soy sauce for an 'elegant' look (as it is not too dark).

If your sauce gets lumpy when you add the potato starch, mix it with a whisk to make it smooth.

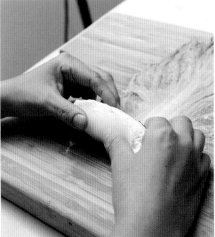

You can use the tofu mixture as fake fish. Spread the tofu onto nori like unagi don (see the recipe for the Unagi Donburi) and pan fry; eat with salt and pepper or your favourite sauce.

Rolled Chinese Cabbage with Tofu Fish and Japanese Broth

Salt and Pepper Tofu

This is my partner's favourite dish. He prefers the firm tofu version so please choose the tofu that you enjoy!

600g (21oz) silken firm or firm tofu

Flour mixture
1 tablespoon black and white peppercorns
1 tablespoon sea salt
2 tablespoons wholemeal flour
2 tablespoons cornflour (cornstarch)

Garnish
Coriander
Red chilli
Lime
Natural oil for frying

1.   Drain the tofu lightly by letting it stand on a tilted chopping board for 10 to 20 minutes.

2.   With a pestle and mortar pound the peppercorns with salt.

3.   Place pepper and salt in a plastic bag and crush with a rolling pin over the bag.

4.   Add the wholemeal and cornflour and mix very well. If you don't mix well in this stage, your tofu won't have an even taste. Some parts would be salty, some parts tasteless.

5.   Toss tofu lightly in the flour mixture and shake off excess. Heat oil in a frying pan over a high heat. When oil is hot, deep-fry tofu, a few pieces at a time, until it is golden. Drain tofu on absorbent paper.

6.   To serve, place tofu on plate with chopped chilli, coriander and lime.

Tip: You can use black peppercorn only, but I like to use a mix of several types of peppercorns. You can purchase a jar of mixed peppercorns at the shops or supermarkets.

Gluten-free option: Use rice flour or potato flour instead of wholemeal flour. They are both very nice. I actually like a potato flour and rice flour mixture the best.

Makes 30

Tofu Spanakopita

Spanakopita is Greek spinach pastry. No egg or cheese is used in this recipe, unlike more traditional recipes. Adding lemon juice and tofu makes the mixture nice and moist. You can also make one big pie instead of making mini triangles.

1 small onion (80g/2½oz), chopped finely
1 bunch silverbeet leaves (swiss chard)
2 tablespoons chopped fresh flat-leaf parsley
½ teaspoon chopped fresh dill
2 tablespoons olive oil
1 teaspoon salt
150g (5oz) firm tofu, crumbled
1 teaspoon lemon juice
100g (3½oz) fillo pastry
non-hydrogenated non-dairy butter, for brushing

1. Preheat oven to 190°C (375°F).

2. Clean and blanch the silverbeet. Strain it very well and shred.

3. Heat 1 tablespoon oil in a saucepan, add the onion, and fry for 5 to 10 minutes, until softened. Add crumbled tofu, salt and lemon juice and fry well. It is important to fry well to get rid of excess water from tofu in this stage. Once all the water is evaporated, add another 1 tablespoon oil, spinach and herbs and sauté further. Season to taste if required.

4. To make triangles, melt the butter.

5. Take out fillo stack from a box and cover with a dampened kitchen towel. Take the fillo sheet from the stack and brush with melted butter. Top with another fillo sheet. Cut buttered fillo stack into 6 strips.

6. Put a heaped teaspoon of filling near 1 corner of a strip on the end nearest to you, then fold the corner of the fillo over to enclose filling and form a triangle. Please see the diagram below.

7. When you close the end, apply a little of the melted butter to the edge and seal it up. Put triangle, seam side down, on a buttered baking tray and brush top with butter.

8. Bake triangles in the middle of the oven until golden brown, 15 to 25 minutes, then cool them slightly.

Tips: For vegetarians, use butter or egg to brush the pastry.

Gluten-free option: Use gluten-free pastry sheets.

Tofu and Basil Bruschetta

This bruschetta features a protein-rich pesto. Make this creamy and crunchy pesto by adding tofu and walnuts. I love to add lots of nuts—nuts give extra nutritional value, flavour and texture. I also like to use pine nuts, like traditional pesto. Pine or cashew nuts give creaminess, whereas walnuts add crunchiness. Of course, this recipe is also perfect for adding to pesto pasta.

Pesto
200g (7oz) firm tofu or silken firm tofu
30g (1oz) basil, chopped roughly
½ teaspoon salt
1 tablespoon extra virgin olive oil
40g (1½oz) walnuts, crushed or chopped roughly

Garnish
4 pieces of wholemeal bread or gluten-free
  bread
6 to 8 cherry tomatoes, sliced
Freshly ground pepper

1. Remove excess water from tofu by boiling or let stand with weight for 30 minutes.

2. Put the basil, tofu, salt and olive oil in a mini food processor and blend until smooth. Add walnuts and blend further. Please do not over blend, so you can enjoy a little crunchiness.

3. Toast the breads.

4. Spread the pesto on the toasted bread. Arrange the tomatoes on top.

5. Serve with freshly ground pepper.

Tip: This tofu basil pesto is great for pasta. To make enough pesto for pasta to serve 4 people, make three batches. Serve with chopped fresh tomato.

Tofu and Okara Nuggets

Before I became a vegetarian, I used to make a tofu and chicken mince nuggets recipe for my cooking class. I then noticed that all other recipes I created for my Tofusion cooking class were vegetarian, and so I decided to make the nuggets totally vegetarian. I substituted chicken with okara and added vegetable stock. It went very well. Seriously, it tastes almost the same as the chicken version.

250g (9oz) okara
½ onion, finely grated
½ potato, finely grated
250g (9oz) hard tofu, crumbled finely by hand
3 tablespoons potato starch
2 teaspoons MSG-free vegetable stock powder
Pinch of nutmeg
Pinch of salt and pepper

Honey mustard
1½ tablespoons honey
1 tablespoon Dijon mustard

1. To make honey mustard, combine the honey and mustard.

2. Place the rest of the ingredients in a bowl and, using your hands, mix until well combined. Shape tablespoons of mixture into nuggets.

3. Heat oil in a saucepan over a high heat. When oil is hot, deep-fry the nuggets until golden.

4. Drain the nuggets on absorbent paper.

5. Serve with honey mustard and sweet chilli sauce

Vegan option: For a vegan alternative, use agave syrup instead of honey.

Two Kinds of Crispy Tofu Sticks

This fantastic finger food is perfect for your next party. It is really easy, yet you will still impress your guests. It's like a thin spring roll with no need to deep fry, and is still crispy.

Tofu and Shiitake Stick

100g (3½oz) shiitake mushroom, sliced thinly
130g (4½oz) hard tofu
8 spring roll wrappers
1 tablespoon sesame oil
½ teaspoon sea salt
Extra sesame oil for brushing

1. Preheat the oven to 200°C (400°F).

2. Crumble the tofu by hand into a bowl. Add sesame oil and salt. Mix well.

3. Place the sliced shiitake, followed by the tofu mixture, down the front of the spring roll sheet. Fold over one end to make a base then roll until the end.

4. Brush the extra sesame oil on the surface of the rolls.

5. Bake for 7 to 10 minutes or until golden and crispy.

Tofu, Cheese and Nori stick

8 spring roll wrappers
160g (5½oz) hard tofu
80g (2½oz) dairy-free cheese
4 sheets nori, cut into half
¼ teaspoon sea salt
Sesame oil for brushing

1. Preheat the oven to 200°C (400°F).

2. Crumble the tofu by hand into a bowl. Add salt and mix well.

3. Place the nori sheet then the tofu mixture down the front of the spring roll sheet. Fold over one end to make a base then roll until the end

4. Brush the extra sesame oil on the surface of the rolls.

5. Bake for 7 to 10 minutes or until golden and crispy.

Tip: Use pizza cheese or shredded mozzarella cheese, in place of dairy-free cheese.

Gluten-free option: Use gluten-free pastry sheets.

Tofu Gyoza

Gyoza is a Japanese dumpling. Shaping gyoza can be tiring so throw a 'gyoza' party with friends and you can shape gyoza and eat together. You can grill, deep-fry or steam them. Adding them into a hot pot is my favourite thing to do. Basic gyoza are made from pork mince, but by adding lots of flavour and texture, tofu gyoza are super tasty.

Filling
250g (9oz) hard tofu
1 cabbage leaf (about 150g/5oz)
2 dried shiitake mushroom, soak in water and remove the stalks, chopped roughly
½ cup tinned bamboo shoots
½ cup tinned water chestnuts
1 small garlic clove, finely grated
1 tablespoon ginger, finely grated
2 stalks shallot, chopped roughly
1½ tablespoons vegetarian mushroom oyster sauce
2 teaspoons soy sauce
2 tablespoons potato starch
1½ packets gow gee wrapper (1 packet approx. 30 to 35 wrappers)
Neutral oil for frying

Dipping sauce
Soy sauce
Rice vinegar
Mix a 1:2 ratio of soy sauce to rice vinegar and add some *layu* (chilli oil) if you like that.

1. Break the tofu into a food processor and process.

2. To get rid of water from tofu, dry fry the processed tofu without any oil (optional) and place in a bowl.

3. Process the cabbage and squeeze out the excess water. Add the cabbage to tofu.

4. Mix the remaining ingredients, except for the potato starch, and process. Add in tofu and cabbage and mix well. Sprinkle the potato starch and mix well with a spoon.

5. Shape and cook the gyoza (see the 'How to' sections following). Serve with dipping sauce.

Gluten-free option: Use rice paper instead.

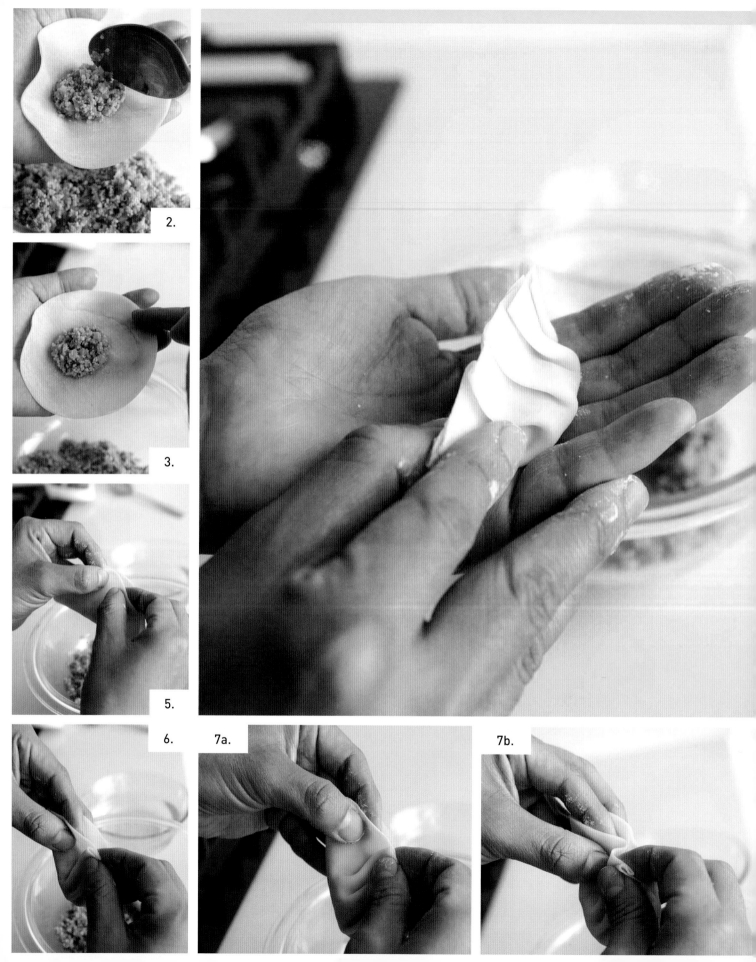

How to shape gyoza

1. Have a small bowl of cold water ready.

2. Lay a gow gee wrapper on your left hand, and place a heaped teaspoon of the mixture in the center of the wrapper.

3. With a fingertip moistened with water, trace a line along half of the edge of the round wrapper.

4. Fold the wrapper over to enclose the filling, and pinch the wrapper in the center to seal the edges together at that spot.

5. Holding the wrapper in that middle spot that you just pinched with your left hand, make a pleat in the top part of the wrapper, pinching it against the flat edge of the wrapper at the back.

6. Holding the filled half-circle in the left hand, pleat the top of the wrapper from the middle out, pressing it to the flat edge of the wrapper at the back (only the front edge will be pleated—the back edge stays flat). Proceed to make two or three more pleats to the right of the first pleat.

7. Switch sides and pleat the other side (to the left of the pinched middle).

8. Set aside the stuffed dumpling with the pleated-wrapper edge up.

9. Repeat the process until all your wrappers have been filled and pleated.

10. Place all gyoza onto floured plates or trays.

How to cook gyoza

1.   In a large skillet with a tight fitting lid, heat 1 teaspoon of the oil over a medium-high heat.

2.   Carefully place as many of the dumplings that can fit without touching on the skillet with the pleated-wrapper edge up.

3.   Cook the dumplings for 3 minutes, or until nicely browned on the bottom. Check the progress by lifting 1 or 2 dumplings up by their pleated edge.

4.   Once the bottoms are nicely browned, use the skillet lid to shield yourself and carefully pour water so that the gyoza are in the water to about half of their height. Place the lid on top.

5.   Maintain the high heat and cook for about 7 minutes. If there is still water in the pan, take off the lid and cook until water is completely vaporised.

6.   If the wrappers are not translucent, pour extra water and put lid on skillet to cook further.

How to keep un-cooked gyoza

*In the fridge for cooking within a week.

Arrange gyoza without pieces touching on baking paper to avoid sticking and cover with wrap.

*In freezer

In a metal tray (freeze quickly to keep the freshness), put gyoza without pieces touching onto baking paper and cover. Once gyoza has frozen, put in a bag.

Cook dumplings until brown.

Pour in water.

Put on a lid to steam.

Tofu Ricotta and Mozzarella

Make interesting ricotta and mozzarella cheese-like recipes using tofu. If you eat it as it is, it tastes like mozzarella; if cooked, it's actually like cooked ricotta. It is much healthier than cheese. There's no dairy and by adding kuzu you get extra health benefits.

300g (10½oz) firm tofu
200ml (7fl oz) soymilk
40g (1½oz) kuzu
¼ teaspoon sea salt
2 teaspoons extra virgin olive oil

1. Place all ingredients except oil in a blender and blend well.

2. Place the mixture in a medium-sized pot and cook over a low heat. Stir constantly.

3. When the mixture gets thick, add the olive oil and turn off the heat.

4. Line ramekins with plastic wrap and then pour the mixture inside.

5. Gather the plastic wrap and twist the top, then place the sealed tofu, still in the ramekin, in the fridge.

To serve as Insalata Caprese

1. Slice some tomatoes.

2. Slice the tofu mozzarella.

3. Sprinkle sea salt on both mozzarella and tomato.

4. Drizzle on some extra virgin olive oil and crack some black pepper.

5. Garnish with basil leaves.

Tip: This cheese is also great to put on crackers and works well in a variety of other exciting recipes, such as the Tofu Ricotta, Mushroom and Spinach Pie and the Tofu Ricotta Pasta

Tofu Tomato Marinade

Grate fresh tomato onto tofu with basil. This makes a fantastic summer delight!

1 tube tofu
2 ripened large tomatoes

Marinade
1 tablespoon extra virgin oil
1 tablespoon lemon juice
¼ teaspoon sea salt
Some pepper

Garnish
Some small basil leaves

1. To remove the excess water from tofu, place enough water to cover the tofu in a small pan and bring to the boil. Place the tofu gently into the pot, and reduce the heat and simmer for 10 minutes. Drain and set aside.

2. When the tofu is cool, slice the tofu into 1cm (¼in) slices and place onto the plate.

3. Combine all marinade ingredients in a bowl.

4. Pour the marinade over the tofu and place in a fridge.

5. Just before serving, grate the tomato onto the tofu and sprinkle over the basil leaves.

Tip: You can use 1 packet of silken tofu (about 300g/10½oz) instead of tube tofu.

Tofu Ricotta and Mozzarella

SIDES

Arame and Edamame Salad

This colourful salad is the perfect way to eat seaweed and fresh vegetables. Enjoy the crunchy texture of veggies, edamame and soft arame, which is full of flavour.

50g (1¾oz) dried arame
200g (7oz) shelled edamame
2 tablespoons extra virgin olive oil
2 teaspoons garlic, chopped
2 teaspoons ginger, chopped
3 tablespoons soy sauce
1 red capsicum (bell pepper), sliced thinly
100g (3½oz) green beans, sliced
80ml (2½fl oz) lemon juice
Pinch of chilli pepper (optional)
200ml (7fl oz) water
1 lettuce, washed

1. Soak the arame in water for at least 10 minutes and then drain.

2. Pour some boiling water over frozen edamame and then drain.

3. Heat the olive oil in a large frying pan over a low heat.

4. Add the garlic and ginger, and gently fry for about 3 minutes, or until the garlic is just beginning to colour. Take care not to let it burn.

5. Add arame and sauté for 2 minutes over a medium-high heat then add soy sauce and the 200ml (7fl oz) amount of water, and cook until all the liquid is nearly gone.

6. Place the cooked arame, vegetables, lemon juice and chilli pepper in a bowl and mix well.

7. Serve with lettuce.

Gluten-free option: Use tamari instead of soy sauce.

Serves 4

Baby Spinach and Tofu Salad with Sweet Basil Dressing

This is one of the most popular dishes in my cooking classes. The sweet basil dressing is very refreshing with lots of flavours and textures from the toppings.

40g (1½oz) pine nuts
200g (7oz) hard tofu
¼ red onion, thinly sliced
200g (7oz) baby spinach
100g (3½oz) sun-dried tomato, sliced

Dressing
30g (1oz) basil leaves
120ml (4fl oz) extra virgin olive oil
120ml (4fl oz) white wine vinegar
½ teaspoon sea salt
3 teaspoons unrefined sugar

1. To toast the pine nuts, spread them on a baking tray and place them in a preheated oven at 180°C (350°F) for 5 to 10 minutes or until golden. Stir once.

2. To dry roast them, cook (without oil) in a large frying pan over a medium heat until golden. Stir constantly and then set aside.

3. To make the dressing, put basil, olive oil, white vinegar, salt and sugar in a blender and blend well.

4. Crumble the tofu by hand into a bowl, add the red onion, sliced sun-dried tomato and half of the dressing. Mix well.

5. Place the baby spinach in a bowl and pour over the rest of the dressing. Toss well. Top with the tofu mixture and pine nuts.

Beetroot, Apple, Carrot, Walnuts and Tofu Salad

This is a delicious winter salad. The tofu also becomes pink so nobody will notice there is tofu in the salad. Crunchy, soft, nutty, sweet—this recipe is full of various textures and flavours.

1 raw beetroot (150g/5oz), grated
1 carrot (100g/3½oz), grated
1 apple (100g/3½oz), grated
150g (5oz) hard tofu, grated
2 tablespoons lemon juice
1 tablespoon grapeseed oil or any neutral tasting oil
¼ teaspoon sea salt
40g (1½oz) walnuts, roasted and crushed
2 teaspoons honey

Garnish
Some chopped parsley

1. Mix all the ingredients together.

2. You can add honey if the apple is not sweet enough.

3. Garnish with chopped parsley and serve.

Tip: You can also add beetroot leaves and stems. To add them, boil and chop them finely.

Vegan version: Use agave syrup or rice syrup instead of honey.

Brown Rice, Edamame and Ume Rice Ball

Rice balls are a typical Japanese lunch. I am very surprised to meet many people who have been to Japan and are crazy about these rice balls. Although, I shouldn't really be surprised, since my idea of the perfect 'last meal' is a white rice ball with ume and nori—that is how much I love rice balls. This version uses brown rice for an even healthier alternative!

2 cups medium-grain brown rice
4 tablespoons (80g/2½oz) shelled frozen
   edamame
2 tablespoons roasted, grained white sesame
   seeds
2 or 3 umeboshi (Japanese salted plum),
   deseeded and broken into small pieces
Some sea salt
Nori, optional

1. Wash the brown rice.

2. Cook the brown rice with a pressure cooker or pot.

3. Once the rice is cooked, place all the ingredients, except salt, in a bowl and mix well.

4. To shape a rice ball, wet your hands and rub them with sea salt.

5. Take ⅙ of the rice and place in your hands. Hold the rice between your palms.

6. Working rapidly, form the rice into a triangular shape, by cupping your hand sharply to form each corner, and keep turning it until you are happy with the shape.

7. Repeat with the rest of the rice.

Tip: Wrap the rice ball with 1–2 strips of nori seaweed if you like that.

Tofu Thin Bread

This is protein-rich bread! It's yeast free, which means there is no need for proving. You can also use this dough for a pizza base. Just bake the dough first then put your favourite toppings on and bake again.

300g (10½oz) silken tofu or silken firm (1 packet)
120 to 130g (4–4½oz) wholemeal flour
3 teaspoons baking powder
30ml (1fl oz) olive oil
¼ teaspoon sea salt
¼ teaspoon unrefined sugar

Garlic butter
50g (1¾oz) non-hydrogenated non-dairy butter
1 teaspoon minced garlic
Your favourite herbs, chopped
(eg parsley, oregano, dill, basil)

1. Break the tofu and boil for 2 minutes and drain. Place a heavy weight on top and let it stand for 2 hours or even overnight, or until the weight of tofu drops to between 120–130g (4–4½oz).

2. If your tofu is more than 130g, add the same amount of flour as tofu (in weight). If your tofu weight is 150g (5oz) for example, you can add 150g (5oz) flour.

3. Place the tofu in a bowl and add the olive oil. Whisk it until smooth, or process it in a small food processor.

4. In a different bowl, place the flour, baking powder, salt and sugar and mix well; then add the tofu mixture and mix together.

5. Tip the dough onto a lightly floured work surface and knead.

6. You may need to add extra flour at this stage if the dough is still a little bit wet. Once the dough is smooth, cover it with plastic wrap and rest in a fridge for 30 minutes. If you are in a hurry, you can move to the next step. Resting in the fridge just makes it a little easier to roll out.

7.   Preheat oven to 200°C (400°F). Place an oven shelf in the lowest position.

8.   Meanwhile, make garlic butter. Place non-dairy butter, minced garlic and herbs, in a small bowl and mix well.

9.   Brush a round pizza tray with olive oil (extra) to lightly grease. Sprinkle with a little flour (extra); this will help the bread become dry with a crisp base. A pizza tray with holes is ideal.

10. Roll out the dough to form a round pizza base and spread with garlic butter.

11. Bake in the preheated oven for 15 minutes. If you like a crispy texture, you can bake for a further 5–10 minutes.

Tip: If you use butter instead of non-dairy butter, soften the butter at room temperature then add garlic and herbs. Mix well.

You can make herbal oil by using 60ml (2fl oz) olive oil instead of 50g (1¾oz) non-dairy butter.

You can prepare this dough the night before and bake the next morning.

Two Kinds of Soymilk Rice

Corn, Millet and Soymilk Rice

This lovely yellow rice is slightly sweet.
The sweetness comes from the corn and
soymilk. Soymilk also gives richness to the
rice. It is a wonderful accompaniment to a
curry or stew.

¾ cup white medium grain rice
¼ cup millet
1 corn
¾ cup water
¾ soymilk
½ teaspoon sea salt

1. Wash the rice and millet separately (see
the Quinoa Inari Sushi recipe for a detailed
description of how to wash the rice).

2. Remove the husk, silk and stem from the
corn. Ensure the corn is stable on the board;
then take the corn kernels off the cob with a
knife then, at an angle, just come in between the
kernels and the cob with your knife, and gently
follow it all the way down, it is almost like in a
sawing motion.

3. Place all the ingredients in a saucepan and
put the lid on. Bring to the boil over a high heat
then turn down to low. Cook for a further
10 minutes. Remove the pan completely from
the heat and leave to stand for a further 10
minutes before removing the lid and serving.

Quinoa, Carrot and Soymilk Rice

Carrot and soymilk add sweetness to the rice. Quinoa adds nutritional value and also makes the rice light. People who don't like quinoa often prefer it when mixed with rice.

^{2}/$_3$ cup white medium grain rice
^{1}/$_3$ cup quinoa
100g (3½oz) carrot, grated
½ teaspoon sea salt
¾ cup soymilk
½ cup water

1.   Wash rice and quinoa separately (see the Quinoa Inari Sushi recipe for a detailed description as to how to wash the rice).

2.   Place all the ingredients in a saucepan and put the lid on. Bring to the boil over a high heat then turn down to low. Cook for a further 10 minutes.

3.   Remove the pan completely from the heat and leave to stand for a further 10 minutes before removing the lid and serving.

Creamy Shiroae

Spinach with creamy tofu and sesame dressing

Shiroae is a traditional Japanese salad. Traditionally, tofu is broken roughly but I put it in a processor to make it creamy so it looks and tastes better! This salad has much less sugar than other recipes.

1 bunch English spinach
2 teaspoons soy sauce
½ (50g) carrot, shredded
½ sheet konnyaku

Dressing

½ (150g) x block silken tofu
2 tablespoons hulled tahini
 2 teaspoons unrefined sugar
1 tablespoon miso

1.   Wrap tofu in cheesecloth or paper towels, and place on a tilted chopping board and let stand for 10 minutes or more to remove excess water.

2.   Wash the spinach and separate the stalks and leaves.

3.   Place the spinach stalks in a saucepan of boiling water and cook for 30 seconds, add the leaves and cook for 10 seconds, then drain and squeeze any excess liquid from spinach. Chop into bitesize pieces. Pour soy sauce over spinach and toss well.

4.   Boil the shredded carrot for 30 seconds. Slice the konnyaku and sprinkle about 1 teaspoon salt (extra) and knead well. Then boil for 2 minutes and drain to remove water and the smell. Drain.

5.   To make dressing, place the tofu, tahini, sugar and miso and in a food processor and process until smooth. Season with salt if needed. The saltiness of miso varies from brand to brand so you can adjust the taste by using salt.

6.   Place spinach, carrot, konnyaku and dressing together and toss well.

Gluten-free option: Use rice miso not barley miso. Use tamari instead of soy sauce.

Daikon and Edamame Salad with Ume Dressing

No oil is used in this dressing; the natural oil from the sesame gives this salad its richness. Daikon and ume are highly alkaline and this dressing is the perfect accompaniment with deep-fried food.

350g (12oz) daikon
120g (4oz) shelled frozen edamame
2 tablespoons white sesame seeds
¼ teaspoon MSG-free konbu dashi powder
1 tablespoon ume (plum) vinegar

Garnish
½ sheet nori
1 large umeboshi

1.   Peel the daikon and finely julienne.

2.   Pour boiling water onto frozen edamame. Drain and set aside.

3.   Toast the sesame seeds on a dry frying pan on a medium heat until golden. Grind the seeds or bruise with a knife.

4.   For the garnish, finely cut the nori seaweed into 2 to 3cm (¾–1in) long slivers using kitchen scissors. Remove the seed from the umeboshi and chop finely.

5.   Combine the edamame, daikon, sesame seeds, ume (plum) vinegar and konbu dashi powder in a large serving bowl and transfer to individual serving bowls.

6.   Garnish with the nori slivers and chopped umeboshi, then serve.

Tip: Add the nori just before serving, otherwise the nori gets wet and gives unwanted texture.

Edamame Mini Rosti

Rosti is the Swiss-German version of the hash brown. Edamame adds beautiful colour and protein—so enjoy!

1 cup shelled frozen edamame
1kg (2lb 4oz) potato, grated
²/₃ cup rice flour
2 teaspoons salt
Neutral oil, for frying
Cracked pepper

1.   Pour boiling water onto shelled edamame and drain well.

2.   Dry the grated potato lightly with a clean tea towel. But retain a little moisture to mix in the rice flour later.

3.   Place grated potato, edamame, rice flour and salt and mix well.

4.   Heat half the oil and butter in a large frying pan over a medium-high heat.

5.   Place a handful of mixture into the pan. Flatten slightly with a spatula to 10cm (4in) in diameter. Repeat this process with the remaining mixture.

6.   Cook for 6 minutes on each side or until golden.

7.   Remove and drain off any excess oil on kitchen paper. Sprinkle a little salt and cracked pepper on top.

Serves 4

Fennel and Baby Spinach Salad with Lemony Chia and Aburaage Dressing

Chia seeds make dressings nice and thick. The sponge-like aburaage absorbs the flavour of the dressing and adds great texture to the salad.

1 medium fennel, thinly sliced
100g (3½oz) baby spinach
1 medium-sized avocado, sliced

Lemony dressing
2 tablespoons chia seeds
150ml (5fl oz) water
2 tablespoons rice vinegar
2 tablespoons lemon juice
2 tablespoons extra virgin olive oil
1 teaspoon sea salt
2 aburaage (refer to 'How to handle deep-fried tofu')

1. To make the dressing, soak the chia seeds with 3 tablespoons water and set them aside.

2. Place rice vinegar, lemon juice, olive oil and salt in a small bowl and mix well.

3. Wash the aburaage with hot water to get rid of oil.

4. Heat the non-stick frying pan and cook the aburaage until crispy (see picture below) on both sides.

5. Cut into thin pieces.

6. Place the crispy aburaage and soaked chia seeds into the lemon mixture.

7. Place the fennel and spinach into a salad bowl, pour over the dressing and mix well.

Quinoa Inari Sushi

This recipe is much healthier than traditional inari sushi. I add quinoa to make the rice light and nutritious. Traditional inari uses much more sugar and soy sauce, but I have cut it down to the bare minimum.

Sushi rice
¾ cup white medium-grain rice
¼ cup quinoa
1 cup water
1 tablespoon white sesame seeds
1 tablespoon black sesame seeds
2½ tablespoons sushi vinegar (or use recipe below)

Inari
5 slices aburaage (refer to 'How to handle deep-
    fried tofu')
1 cup water
1 teaspoon instant dashi powder
2 tablespoons mirin
1 tablespoon unrefined sugar
1 tablespoon soy sauce

Garnish
Pickled ginger

1. To make the rice, wash the rice in a small amount of water using a kneading-like action with the palm of the hand. Drain and repeat the process until the water is almost clear. Wash quinoa with running water. Place water and rice and quinoa in a saucepan or rice cooker and leave to stand for 20 to 30 minutes before cooking. Alternatively, cook the rice and quinoa using the absorption method if not using a rice cooker.

2. Toast the white sesame seeds in a dry frying pan on medium heat until golden. Set aside. Repeat with the black sesame seeds until they have a slightly glossy appearance. Keeping the black and white sesame seeds separate, grind the seeds or bruise with a knife.

3. When the rice is cooked and while still hot, slowly add the sushi vinegar and stir through well. Using a handheld fan, cool the rice as quickly as possible.

4. Spoon half the cooked rice into a separate bowl and mix in the toasted white sesame seeds. Combine the remaining cooked rice with the toasted black sesame seeds. Cover the rice with paper towel and set aside.

5. To make the inari, place the aburaage slices into a saucepan with enough boiling water to cover and boil for 2 to 3 minutes. (Refer to the How to handle deep-fried tofu section in the Introduction).

6. Drain well and rinse the aburaage under running water to remove excess oil. Gently squeeze out any of the remaining liquid.

On a cutting board, carefully roll out each slice of aburaage with a rolling pin or round chopsticks taking care not to roll it too thinly. Cut each piece of aburaage in half to make 2 squares. Using your fingers and beginning at the cut end, gently separate the sides of each square to form a pouch.

7. Place 1 cup of water and the dashi powder in a medium saucepan and bring to the boil. Reduce the heat and add the mirin and sugar, stirring well. Add in the aburaage pouches and simmer gently over the low heat for 5 minutes or until the liquid is reduced by half. Pour in the soy sauce, distributing it evenly by carefully rotating the saucepan over the heat.

8. Closely cover the mixture with baking paper and simmer on low heat until all the liquid is absorbed. (For best results, allow the aburaage to marinate overnight in the liquid in the refrigerator.) When cool, drain off any excess liquid.

9. With wet hands, form the rice and white sesame seed mixture into 5 evenly sized balls. Repeat with the remaining rice and black seed mixture.

10. Carefully stuff one rice ball into each aburaage pocket, pressing the rice mixture firmly into the pouch to distribute evenly. Fold over the open ends to seal the pouch.

11. Press lightly to shape and place the folded side down on a serving dish. Garnish with pickled ginger.

Healthy Sushi Vinegar
30ml (1fl oz) brown rice vinegar or rice vinegar
¼ teaspoon salt
1 teaspoon unrefined sugar
1 tablespoon mirin

1. To make Healthy Sushi Vinegar, simply mix the ingredients together well.

Gluten-free option: Use tamari instead of soy sauce.

Tip: You can simply use plain vinaigrette rice instead of adding sesame. It is also very nice to add simmered carrot and shiitake to the rice. Both ways are also very popular in Japan.

Tofu and Wakame Salad with Japanese Sesame Dressing

This thick Japanese style of dressing is my absolute favourite! I'm actually not a big fan of salad but I can eat lots of salad with this dressing. When preparing it, do not be scared to cut the tofu on your palm! It will help you keep the shape of the tofu.

1 packet (300g (10½oz) silken tofu
200g (7oz) mixed salad leaves
2 tablespoons dried wakame
½ teaspoon sesame oil
pinch of salt

Sesame dressing
2 tablespoons white sesame
2 tablespoons onion, roughly chopped
2 tablespoons carrot, roughly chopped
1 small clove garlic, grated finely
½ cup neutral oil
2 tablespoons brown rice or rice vinegar
60ml (2fl oz) soy sauce
1 tablespoon unrefined sugar

Gluten-free option: Use tamari instead of soy sauce.

1. Leave silken tofu on a plate or strainer for half an hour to drain naturally.

2. To prepare the sesame for dressing, toast the white sesame seeds in a dry frying pan on a medium heat until golden. Cool down and grind. Keep one teaspoon of sesame for wakame.

3. To make the dressing, place the rest of the sesame, chopped onion, carrot, grated garlic, oil, vinegar, soy sauce and sugar in a blender and blend well.

4. To prepare the wakame, place wakame in warm water until reconstituted (soft) and drain. If there are any stalks of wakame, remove it then cut the wakame into small pieces.

5. Heat a frying pan with sesame oil, place wakame in and fry. Add one teaspoon of roasted and ground sesame and a pinch of salt. Set aside.

6.   To serve, place the salad mix in a bowl, then cut the tofu into small cubes on your palm and arrange them around the salad leaves. Arrange the wakame over the top, and then pour dressing over the salad.

Tip: You can keep this dressing for three months in most fridges.

See the picture below for instructions as to cutting tofu on your palm. Silken tofu is quite fragile so if you cut it on a chopping board and try to move it, it will fall apart. Use this technique whenever you cut silken tofu so that it can keep its shape.

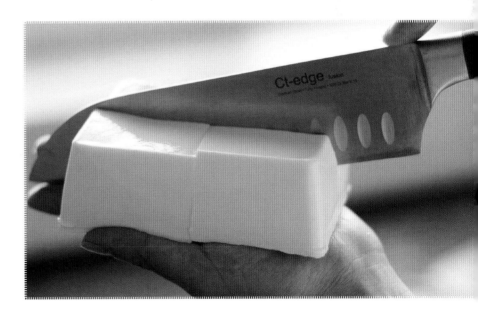

MAINS

Baked Pumpkin with Soy Bechamel

This cute dish features bechamel and 'bean-naise' sauces ('bean-naise' sauce is my own invention—my version of a béarnaise sauce) and is perfect to use when entertaining.

2kg (4lb 8oz) Japanese pumpkin

Super easy gluten and dairy free béchamel
60g (2oz) glutinous rice flour (sweet rice flour)
600ml (21fl oz) soymilk
1 teaspoon MSG-free vegetable stock powder
$2/3$ teaspoon sea salt
Pinch of nutmeg
Pinch of white pepper

Bean-naise sauce
150g (5oz) tomato paste
2 tablespoons red wine
1 tablespoon miso
½ teaspoon sea salt
1 teaspoon soy sauce
1 tablespoon olive oil for frying
1 tin (400g/14oz) red kidney beans
1 garlic clove, minced
½ onion, chopped finely
100g (3½oz) mushroom, chopped finely
60g (2oz) walnuts, chopped finely

Topping
2 tablespoons of your favourite nuts chopped
Soymilk for brushing

1. Preheat the oven to 180°C (350°F).

2. To make the béchamel sauce, put glutinous rice flour into a bowl and add ⅓ of soymilk slowly—mix very well with a whisk.

3. Add the rest of the soymilk and mix.

4. Strain the mixture into a saucepan and heat over a medium heat. Add the stock powder, sea salt, nutmeg and pepper, stir occasionally and cook until thick.

5. To make bean-naise sauce, mix together the tomato paste, red wine, miso, sea salt and soy sauce then set aside.

1. Heat oil in a large frying pan over a medium heat. Add garlic and onion and sauté until soft. Add mushroom and walnuts and cook further until mushroom is soft and add sauce mixture. Cook until sauce thickens. Set aside.

2. Next, use a sharp knife to remove the top of the pumpkin and set aside. Scrape out and discard the seeds and fibre.

3. Lay a large, lightly oiled sheet of foil over the base and sides of a baking tray and brush with a little olive oil. Place the pumpkin on the tray, putting the bean-naise sauce inside the pumpkin.

4. Place pumpkin lid on top and bring sides of the foil up around pumpkin. Cover top with more lightly oiled foil so pumpkin is completely enclosed. Bake in the oven for 1.5 hours

5. Open the foil and the lid of the pumpkin and pour half of the béchamel sauce on top. Brush on the soymilk and sprinkle the nuts. Put back in the oven and bake for further 30 minutes or until tender (test by piercing the flesh with a skewer).

6. Serve pumpkin and filling as a dish on its own with the rest of the warm béchamel sauce on the side.

Gluten-free option: Use tamari instead of soy sauce and use rice miso, not barley miso.

Colourful Tofu Teriyaki Bowl

The Japanese use soy sauce often, which tends to make meals look very brown. By adding additional colour to your meals, you will encourage kids to eat. You could also add pickled ginger for extra colour. The egg in this recipe is slightly sweet as the Japanese sometimes cook egg with sugar. You will taste it when you eat egg sushi in sushi restaurants!

500g (17½oz) silken firm or firm tofu
Potato starch for dusting
100g (3½oz) green beans
3 tablespoons oil for frying
2 cups of your favourite rice, cooked
- brown rice
- white rice with other grains (see Unagi Donburi and Quinoa Inari recipes)

Teriyaki sauce
2 tablespoons soy sauce
2 tablespoons mirin
1 tablespoon sake
1 tablespoon agave syrup or unrefined sugar

Egg topping
4 free-range eggs
3 tablespoons mirin
½ teaspoon salt

Garnish
Nori sheets, for garnish

1. Place tofu on a tilted chopping board. Let it stand for 10 to 20 minutes.

2. To prepare veggies, clean both sides of the green beans and cut into two then boil or steam them for 3 to 5 minutes or until cooked. Set aside.

3. To prepare egg topping, combine all ingredients.

4. Heat the frying pan with 1 teaspoon of oil and pour egg mixture. Stir consistently (if you can use four chopsticks for mixing, you can make very fine egg crumble). Set aside.

5. To prepare garnish, cut the nori sheet into thin strips using scissors. Set aside.

6. To make teriyaki sauce, combine all ingredients, and then set aside.

7. To cook tofu, cut the tofu into bite size and pat dry with kitchen paper.

8. Toss tofu lightly in potato starch and shake away excess.

9. Heat the frying pan and place the tofu inside; cook over a medium heat until golden on both sides. Turn off the heat.

10. Wipe excess oil onto a pan with kitchen paper.

11. Pour teriyaki sauce and let it boil with residue of heat. Turn tofu to coat it with sauce. Turn on low heat if the sauce is not thick enough at this stage and simmer to thicken the sauce.

12. Place the rice into a bowl then arrange egg, teriyaki tofu and beans onto rice. Pour on rest of teriyaki sauce. Top with shredded nori.

Vegan option: Simply serve without egg.

Gluten-free option: Use tamari instead of soy sauce.

Chargrilled Marinade Tempeh with Avocado Salsa and Summer Quinoa Salad

1 packet (250g/9oz) tempeh

Marinade
½ tablespoon tamari
½ tablespoon olive oil
1 teaspoon Dijion mustard or any mustard of your choice
¼ teaspoon oregano
¼ teaspoon thyme
½ teaspoon lemon juice
Pinch of chili flakes

Avocado salsa
1 large avocado, diced
1 teaspoon extra virgin olive oil
1 teaspoon lemon juice
¼ teaspoon sea salt

Summer quinoa salad
100g (3½oz) quinoa
½ red capsicum (bell pepper), diced
2 Roma tomatoes, diced
1 tablespoon olive oil
1 teaspoon salt
2 teaspoons lemon juice
2 tablespoons parsley, chopped

1. To make the salad, place water in a large pot and bring to the boil. When boiling, add salt, add the quinoa and cook for 10 minutes.

2. Meanwhile, toss the capsicum, tomato, olive oil, salt and lemon juice together.

3. When the quinoa is ready, drain, and add to the salad. Mix well.

4. Add in chopped parsley just before serving.

5. Prepare the tempeh for marinating. Cut the tempeh diagonally into 4 triangles. If possible, thin those triangles out by slicing each in half horizontally—8 triangles in total.

6. Combine marinade ingredients in a bowl, large enough to toss tempeh.

7. Place tempeh in a bowl, toss and distribute the marinade throughout the tempeh. Marinate for at least 30 minutes; feel free to marinate it for 2 days if you want a stronger taste. Be sure to flip occasionally whatever length of time you use.

8. To make the salsa, place olive oil, lemon juice, salt and diced avocado, toss well.

9. Grill the tempeh on a medium-hot grill for a few minutes on each side.

10. Once cooked, serve the tempeh with avocado salsa and the quinoa salad.

Tip: You can use quinoa salad, tempeh and avocado salad as a stuffing for rice paper rolls.

Chargrilled Marinade Tempeh
with Avocado Salsa
and Summer Quinoa Salad

Chargrilled Marinade Tempeh
with Avocado Salsa
and Summer Quinoa Salad, used as
stuffing for rice paper rolls

Cold Olive Pasta

It may not be the best-looking pasta but this tastes great. I was actually amazed by the taste. I didn't add any oil but the sauce is still rich because natural oil comes from the soybeans and olives. You can still drizzle on extra olive oil at the end if you like. You can also warm the sauce and eat it in the winter!

400g (14oz) penne or gluten-free penne
120g (4oz) pitted black olives
300g (10½oz) cooked soybeans
2 tomatoes (280g/10oz), roughly chopped
2 teaspoons sea salt

Garnish
1 tomato, diced
Fresh oregano leaves, to serve

1.   Cook pasta in a saucepan of rapidly boiling water until al dente.

2.   While pasta is cooking, place the soybeans, olive, tomato and salt in a food processor and process until smooth.

3.   Drain pasta and add it to olive mixture.

4.   Toss to combine. To serve, place the pasta on serving bowls and top with fresh diced tomato and oregano. You can drizzle extra virgin olive oil if you wish.

Tip: For a gluten-free option, use gluten-free pasta.

It is also great to eat warm. Just heat up the olive mixture and toss with pasta in a frying pan.

You can also enjoy this mixture as a dip.

Corn, Onion and Edamame Kakiage with Green Tea Salt

Kakiage is a type of tempura made with different ingredients that have been sliced and mixed in a tempura batter. Then a pancake-like shape is made when deep-frying. Traditionally, tempura batter is made from flour, egg and water. It is very hard to make it crispy with the traditional batter but I have made this batter recipe so anybody can make it crispy no matter what version. And it's vegan and gluten-free, which is a fantastic alternative!

1 cob sweet corn
120g (4oz) onion, sliced
100g (3½oz) frozen shelled edamame

Batter
4 tablespoons brown rice or rice flour
4 tablespoons cornflour (cornstarch)
½ teaspoon baking powder
80ml (2½oz) water
Neutral oil for frying

Green tea salt
½ teaspoon green tea powder
2 teaspoon salt flakes

1.   Pour boiling water over frozen edamame. Drain well and pat dry.

2.   Remove the husk, silk and stem from the corn. Then take corn kernel off the cob using a knife. To take the kernels off, you want to have the cob stable on the board. Then on an angle, you come just in between the kernels and the cob with your knife, and gently follow it all the way down, almost like in a sawing motion.

3.   Place edamame, corn and onion in a bowl, then add flour and mix well. Make sure you coat the ingredients well with flour, otherwise oil will splash while deep-frying. Add water and mix well. Divide into 8 to 10 equal parts.

4.   Next, heat the oil in a frying pan over medium heat. The oil will be ready when you drop one small piece of food (like a corn kernel) into the oil and it floats to the surface straight away. If the food floats but gets burnt, the temperature is too hight.

5.   Spoon the divided mixture onto a wooden spoon. Flatten the mixture slightly with a spoon.

6.   Slowly push the mixture into oil. Deep-fry until the edges of the kakiage become golden brown then turn to cook the other side.

7.   Rest on kitchen paper to absorb excess oil.

8.   To make tea salt, combine salt and tea powder.

9.   Serve with tea salt.

Tip: To make carrot, edamame kakiage, use 120g (4oz) thinly chopped carrots instead of corn.

You can serve with tentsuyu (see the Kakiage don recipe). Kakiage can be served with noodle soup (see the Kakiage udon recipe) and donburi (see the Kakiage Bowl recipe).

Both carrot and corn kakiage are pictured.

Corn, Onion and Edamame Kakiage with Green Tea Salt

Creamy Silverbeet and Corn Pasta

You can make rich creamy sauces without dairy! This sauce slightly tastes like cheese and the secret ingredient is white miso. It is also nice to make this pasta with mushrooms, brussel sprouts, turnip, spinach, broccoli, asparagus—any vegetables that go with a creamy sauce.

5 stalks silverbeet (swiss chard)
400g (14oz) fettucine or gluten-free fettucine
2 teaspoons cornflour (cornstarch)
2 teaspoons water
400ml (14fl oz) soymilk
2 tablespoons white miso
4 tablespoons olive oil
2 teaspoons garlic, chopped
Fresh corn kernels from one cob or 1 small tin
1 teaspoon sea salt
Black pepper

1. Using a sharp knife and working from the stem end of the silverbeet towards leaf end, strip leaves from stems. Roughly chop leaves. Trim stems and slice diagonally.

2. Cook pasta in a saucepan of lightly salted boiling water until it is al dente. Add the silverbeet leaves just before you finish cooking the pasta, to blanch.

3. Meanwhile, combine the cornflour and water and set aside.

4. Combine soymilk and white miso and mix well. Set aside.

5. Heat the oil in a frying pan over low heat and add garlic; sauté until you can smell the aroma. Add the silverbeet stalks, corn and salt and cook over medium-high heat for 3 minutes or until the silverbeet is almost cooked.

6. Add the soymilk mixture and bring to the boil. Add the cornflour mixture (mix very well just before adding) and cook until sauce gets thick.

7. Add the pasta and leaves into the pan and toss well.

8. Season to taste.

9. Serve with generous amount of cracked pepper.

Tip: Do not boil the sauce for too long otherwise it will split and lose the miso goodness.

White miso is supposed to be sweet but I have found lots of salty white miso in my travels. Some have the wrong labelling or are simply too old (matured), so check the label before you buy. The tip is to find white miso with a light yellow colour!

If you are not sure which white miso is real, buy *saikyo miso*. It is a bit sweeter than white miso but it is better than unwanted surprises!

Gluten-free option: For a gluten-free option, use gluten-free pasta.

Eggplant Parmigiana

This stuffed eggplant-style parmigiana has hidden tofu, instead of being laden with cheese. I've added a thick creamy soymilk sauce to the mixture so even if you want to use some real parmesan, you don't need to put in too much because of the creamy sauce.

2 eggplants (aubergines) (1kg/2lb 4oz)
1 tablespoon olive oil
2 teaspoons sea salt
Cracked pepper
300g (10½oz) silken firm or firm tofu
120ml (4fl oz) soymilk
1 tablespoon cornflour (cornstarch)
½ onion, finely chopped
4 tomatoes, diced
2 tablespoons parsley, chopped
4 tablespoons dairy-free parmesan cheese

Garnish
Chopped parsley
Cracked pepper

1. Preheat oven to 180°C (350°F).

2. Line an oven tray with baking paper. Cut eggplant in half lengthways.

3. On the bottom of the eggplant, cut a ¼ to ½cm (¼in) thick slice off the rounded apex to make the eggplant shell stable as a dish.

4. Cut a 1cm (½in) border around the inside edge of each half and scoop out the flesh. Chop the eggplant flesh into small pieces and set aside. Brush the eggplant with oil, both inside and on the bottom, and sprinkle with salt and pepper. Bake for 20 minutes or until tender.

5. Meanwhile, place the tofu in a non-stick frying pan and cook over a medium heat. Break the tofu using a wooden spoon and sprinkle with an extra pinch of salt. Cook until the water of the tofu evaporates. Set aside.

6.   Mix 1 tablespoon of soymilk and cornflour.
Set aside.

7.   Heat the oil in the same frying pan over a
medium-low heat. Add the onion and sauté until
soft. Add the reserved eggplant flesh and salt,
and cook, stirring occasionally, for 3 minutes.
Add the tomato, chopped parsley and tofu that
was set aside earlier and cook, stirring for a
further 2 minutes.

8.   Add the rest of the soymilk (100ml/3½fl oz)
into a frying pan and bring to the boil. Add the
soymilk and cornflour mixture (mix well just
before adding) and cook until thickened.

9.   Spoon the mixture evenly among the
eggplant halves. Brush the edges of the
eggplant with some of the extra oil. Sprinkle the
parmesan cheese over the mixture.

10. Bake in the oven for 15 minutes, or until the
eggplant is tender. Serve with chopped parsley
and cracked pepper.

Creamy Tomato Curry with Cheese and Fried Egg

Adding soymilk to a tomato curry base makes it creamy. This curry is full of soybeans and vegetables. Best served with melted cheese and egg!

1 tablespoon oil
1 onion, diced
2 teaspoons garlic, chopped
2 teaspoons ginger, chopped
2 teaspoons curry powder
1 teaspoon turmeric
½ teaspoon cumin powder
2 cups dried soybeans, cooked
2 stalks celery, diced
1 red capsicum, diced
1 carrot, diced
1 cup vegetable stock
3 teaspoons sea salt
400g (14oz) can diced tomatoes
3 bay leaves
100ml (3½fl oz) soymilk
2 cups cooked rice

Garnish
4 free-range eggs
Extra oil for frying egg
160g (5½oz) mozzarella or pizza cheese, thinly sliced
Chopped parsley
Cracked pepper.

1.   Heat the oil in a large saucepan over a medium-low heat.

2.   Add the onion, garlic and ginger then cook until soft and the aroma has come out. Add curry powder, turmeric and cumin powder and sauté for 2 minutes.

3.   Add cooked soybeans and the vegetables and sauté for 2 minutes.

4.   Add vegetable stock, salt, tomato and bay leaf and cook for 20 minutes.

5.   Add the soymilk and simmer for 4 minutes.

6.   To make fried egg with cheese, heat oil in a frying pan and crack the egg. Turn over when the egg is cooked and place some cheese on top of it. Place lid on and cook for a further 2 minutes.

7.   Serve with rice (it is served here with Carrot and Quinoa Rice) topped with fried egg with cheese, chopped parsley and a generous amount of cracked pepper.

Vegan option: Just omit the fried egg and use non-dairy cheese.

Tip: After adding soymilk, do not boil otherwise the curry will start to split.

Edamame Kakiage Bowl

This is one example of how you can enjoy your kakiage or tempura. You can also use this sauce (*tentsuyu*) as a dipping sauce for tempura and kakiage.

Tempura Sauce (*tentsuyu*)
600ml (21lf oz) water
3 tablespoons mirin
1½ teaspoons MSG-free dashi powder
⅓ teaspoon salt
3 tablespoons soy sauce

Kakiage
(see recipe for Corn, Onion and Edamame Kakiage recipe)

This meal is to be served with your favourite rice.
*   Brown rice (see the recipe from Brown Rice, Edamame and Ume Rice Ball)
*   Millet and amaranth rice (see the recipe from Unagi Donburi)
*   Quinoa rice (see the recipe from Inari Quinoa Sushi)

Garnish
Shichimi tougarashi* (optional)

1.   Cook your favourite rice.

2.   Cook kakiage (see the kakiage recipe).

3.   To make the tempura sauce, place all the sauce ingredients, except the soy sauce, in a small saucepan, bring to the boil and keep boiling for 1 minute.

4.   Turn off the heat and add soy sauce.

5.   Place cooked rice in a bowl then place in two pieces of kakiage.

6.   Pour the sauce all over the kakiage and rice.

Tip: Some people like to dip the kakiage or tempura into the sauce first then put it on top of the rice. If you like to enjoy the crispy kakiage, pour the sauce just before serving.

Gluten-free option: Use tamari instead of soy sauce.

Kakiage Udon

This is another way of enjoying your kakiage or tempura. You might not believe that we put crispy tempura in soup to get soggy, but it is very popular in Japan. You can serve kakiage or tempura on the side, which we also do.

1.5 litres (52fl oz) water
1½ tablespoons MSG-free konbu dashi powder
1½ teaspoons salt
1½ tablespoons soy sauce
400g (14oz) dried udon noodles or 4 frozen udon*

Kakiage
(see recipe for Corn, Onion and Edamame
    Kakiage)

Garnish
Chopped shallot (scallion)
Shichimi tougarashi (seven-spice chilli powder) *

1.   Make the kakiage following the recipe instructions.

2.   Place the water and dashi powder in a saucepan and bring to the boil; allow to boil for a further 1 minute.

3.   Add the salt and soy sauce.

4.   To cook dried udon, place the noodles in a large saucepan of boiling water and stir.

5.   Allow water to come back to the boil and then add cold water or reduce heat. Cook

until the udon is soft or follow the package instructions. Then drain. If frozen, just cook for 1 minute in boiling water.

6.   Place the udon in a serving bowl, pour on the soup then place the kakiage on top.

7.   Serve with chopped shallot and shichimi tougarashi.

Tip: I used quinoa udon in this photo. You can also use soba instead of udon.

Gluten-free option: Use rice flour fettuccine or rice noodles and use tamari instead of soy sauce.

Serves 4

Miso Ramen

Slowly cooked ginger, shallot and garlic gives this dish a beautiful seasoning. Adding plenty of sesame makes the soup rich and thick. Enjoy this unbelievably flavoursome soup—perfect for winter.

4 tablespoons sesame oil
3 to 4 (white part of) shallots (scallions), finely chopped
4 tablespoons ginger, chopped
2 tablespoons garlic, chopped
4 fresh shiitake mushrooms, sliced
1.5 litres (52fl oz) water
1 tablespoon MSG-free dashi powder
4 tablespoons roasted and ground sesame seeds
5 to 6 tablespoons miso paste
Salt and pepper, to taste
½ packet bean sprouts
12 snow peas, cleaned and julienned
1 small carrot, julienned
1 small tin corn kernels, drained
1 large red chilli, sliced (optional)
4 bundles of fresh ramen noodles

Garnish
Green shallot (scallion), sliced

Gluten-free option: Use rice miso not barley miso and replace ramen noodles with gluten-free noodles.

Vegan option: Use egg-free ramen noodles.

1. Heat 2 tablespoons of the sesame oil, shallots, ginger and garlic in a large saucepan over a low heat for 4 to 5 minutes to infuse the flavour slowly.

2. Add shiitake mushroom and cook for a further 2 minutes.

3. Add water and dashi powder and bring to the boil. Allow to simmer for 2 minutes and turn off the heat. Add the sesame and miso paste, using a strainer, and season with salt and pepper to your liking.

4. Heat 2 tablespoons of sesame oil in a wok over a high heat and add the bean sprouts, snow peas, carrot, corn and chilli and stir-fry quickly. Season with salt and pepper.

5. Cook the noodles in a separate pan following packet directions, drain and set aside.

6. Add noodles to bowls, pour over broth, top with stir-fried vegetables and chopped shallot.

Tip: I like crunchy vegetables, which is why I stir-fry them in a separate wok, but if you want an easier version, you can add all the vegetables into the soup—less washing up!

Serves 4

Shoyu Ramen (soy-sauce based)

I thought I would have to give up ramen when I became a vegetarian. But I am very happy to tell you that you can make delicious vegetarian ramen soup without MSG (most ramen soup contains MSG) and a shorter cooking time (ramen soup takes hours and hours to make) is POSSIBLE! The key is to cook the ginger and onion very slowly.

4 tablespoons sesame oil
1 tablespoon ginger, finely chopped
1 onion, thinly sliced
1.6 litres (54fl oz) water
1 tablespoon konbu dashi powder
1 teaspoon sea salt
4 tablespoons soy sauce
1 large tofu sheet (yuba)
1 tablespoon sake
1 tablespoon mirin
½ tablespoon soy sauce
4 bunches fresh ramen noodle
Asian greens (bok choy or choy sum)
2 tablespoons dried wakame, soaked in water
   and drained
1 small tin corn kernels

1. To make the soup, heat sesame oil, ginger and onion in a large wok or saucepan over a low heat and cook slowly until onion is cooked.

2. Add water, dashi powder and salt and bring to the boil.

3. Reduce the heat to low and add the soy sauce. Set aside.

4. To cook the tofu sheet, soak the sheet in warm water. Drain and make the tofu roll.

5. Heat the extra sesame oil in the frying pan over a medium-high heat. Place in the rolled tofu sheet and cook until golden on all sides.

6. Add sake and mirin and cook for 1 minute or until evaporated; then add soy sauce and cook for a further 1 minutes, shaking well to coat the sauce. Cut into 8 pieces. Set aside.

7. Cook noodles in a separate pan following packet directions, add Asian greens just before draining the noodles to blanch and set aside.

8. Put noodles in the bowls; pour the broth over them, top with Asian vegetables, tofu sheet, wakame and corn. Serve immediately.

Gluten-free option: Use tamari instead of soy sauce and replace noodles with a gluten-free variety.

Vegan option: Use egg-free ramen noodles.

Nasu No Dengaku

Grilled eggplant with sweet red and white miso sauce

Traditionally, we make this dish by deep-frying. In my version, you can use the oven—it requires much less oil and much less hassle. Enjoy two kinds of sugar-reduced versions of miso sauce and this sauce can be used in other dengaku dishes, such as tofu and konnyaku.

2 medium eggplants oil for brushing

Red miso sauce (Aka dengaku miso)
1 tablespoon haccyo or red miso
1 tablespoon mirin
1 tablespoon sake
3 teaspoons unrefined sugar

Shiro (White) dengaku miso
60g (2oz) white miso
2 tablespoons mirin
1 tablespoon sake
1 teaspoon unrefined sugar

1. Preheat the oven to 250°C (480°F). Line an oven tray with baking paper.

2. To prepare the eggplants, work quickly to prevent the flesh from discolouring. Cut eggplant in half lengthways.

3. On the skin side of the eggplant, cut a 2.5–5mm (¹⁄₈in) thick slice off the rounded apex to form a stable base for the eggplant when preparing and cooking.

4. Cut a 1cm (½in) border around the inside edge of each half. Score the eggplant flesh horizontally and vertically to form a pattern of small but deep squares into the flesh, being careful not to cut the skin. Repeat for each half.

5. Brush the flesh of the eggplants liberally with oil and place on an oven tray in the centre of the oven. Bake for 20 minutes or until the flesh is soft. Remove from the oven.

6. Meanwhile, to make the aka (red) dengaku miso sauce, combine the haccyo miso, mirin and sake in a small saucepan, mixing well to remove any lumps before cooking. While stirring

continuously, bring slowly to the boil over a low heat. Cook gently for a further 2 to 3 minutes or until the sauce begins to thicken, and is smooth and glossy in appearance.

7. To make the shiro (white) dengaku miso sauce, place the miso, mirin, sake and brown sugar in a small saucepan. Cook over low heat as per the red miso sauce instructions.

8. When the eggplant is cooked, spoon the shiro (white) sauce lengthwise over one half of the patterned squares using the centre incision as a guide. Spoon the aka (red) sauce over the remaining half of the pattern. Repeat for each eggplant portion.

Tip: Grill the eggplants for 5 minutes on a medium heat keeping the top of the eggplant away from the grilling element to prevent the sauce burning.

Try to find white miso with a light yellow colour. If you are not sure which white miso to buy, get *saikyo miso*. It is a bit sweeter than white miso and will work very well here.

Gluten-free option: Make sure to use rice miso, not barley miso.

Spaghetti Tofu and Celery Peperoncino

Spaghetti Aglio, Olio, e Peperoncino (Spaghetti garlic, oil, and hot chilli pepper) is my favourite pasta. Adding tofu and celery makes this pasta more substantial and nutritious. I use celery leaves instead of Italian parsley. Many people throw away celery leaves so please try it this way; the leaf tastes quite similar to parsley!

600g (21oz) firm tofu
4 dried whole chillies
6 stalks of celery, with leaves
400g (14oz) spaghetti or gluten-free spaghetti
5 tablespoons olive oil
Sea salt
4 cloves garlic, sliced
Cracked pepper

1. Break the tofu into bite sizes and let it stand on a strainer for 10 minutes.

2. Slice 1 dried chilli and remove the seeds. If you don't like it too spicy, do not chop the chilli (it will be less spicy when not chopped).

3. Trim the leaves from the celery. Shred the leaves roughly. Slice the stalk thinly at an angle (in a diagonal movement).

4. Cook pasta in a saucepan of lightly salted boiling water until it is al dente. Reserve a full ladle of salted water ready to use later.

5. While pasta is cooking, heat 1 tablespoon of oil in a large frying pan over medium heat and add the tofu. Cook, not stirring for 5 minutes or until golden. Add sliced celery and a good pinch of salt and stir for 2 minutes. Set aside.

6. Heat the rest of the oil and garlic in the same saucepan over a low heat and cook until the garlic turns nearly pale gold, it takes about 5 to 7 minutes (do not let the garlic turn brown, otherwise the sauce will taste bitter). Add chopped and whole chillies and cook for another minute.

7. Drain the pasta and add it to the hot garlic and oil mixture with the reserved salted water. Toss to combine then put back the tofu and celery. Add celery leaves at the end and season with salt.

8. Serve with a generous sprinkling of black pepper.

Spaghetti Tofu and Celery Peperoncino

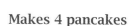

Okara Okonomiyaki

This is a Japanese savoury pancake. Okonomi means 'as you like', so you can put on whatever toppings you want. Pork and seafood are very popular toppings, or you could add corn, cheese or tofu—just use this recipe as a base. These pancakes normally use flour and egg but I have created this egg and gluten-free version—the texture is surprisingly similar.

Pancake mixture
2 eggs (you can use ground flaxseed or an egg
    replacer instead, see tip below)
120ml (4fl oz) water
40g (1½oz) rice flour
80g (2½oz) potato flour
100g (3½oz) cabbage, finely chopped
Pinch of salt
100g (3½oz) okara
Oil for frying

Garnish
Okonomiyaki sauce
Egg-free mayonnaise or Japanese mayonnaise
Benisyouga (optional)
Aonori (optional)

1. Place eggs and water in a bowl and mix well.

2. Add rice flour, potato flour, cabbage, salt and okara and mix well.

3. Heat the oil in a frying pan on a medium heat and pour in half of the mixture. When the edge of the pancake looks dry, turn it over and cook until golden.

4. Pour the okonomiyaki sauce on the pancake.

5. Serve with mayonnaise, benisyouga and aonori.

Tip: Add any toppings—try tofu, cheese, corn, carrot, shallot or your favourite vegetables.

Vegan option: Replace the egg with ground flaxseed. Place 30g (1oz) ground flaxseed and 90ml (3fl oz) water in a food processor or blender and process until it is a thick and creamy consistency. Then stir in 200ml (7fl oz) water instead of 120ml (4fl oz) water. You can whip by hand instead of using a mini food processor but a food processor is much easier and gives a better outcome. Or you can use egg replacer. Simply follow the instructions on the packet. Using a whisk, mix all ingredients, except cabbage, for the pancake mixture, then add cabbage and mix.

Okara Sausage

This is very easy to make. Just mix together all the ingredients and steam. Kids will love it.

1 cup okara
½ cup potato starch
70ml (2½fl oz) soymilk
2 tablespoons olive oil
Pinch of dried thyme
2 tablespoons tomato sauce (ketchup)
½ teaspoon garlic, grated
¼ teaspoon sea salt
Cracked pepper
1 teaspoon Worcestershire sauce (optional)
Oil for frying

1. Place all the ingredients, except the oil, in a bowl and mix well. Divide the mixture into four.

2. Cut some baking paper into 4 pieces (A4 size).

3. Place the mixture onto the baking sheet and shape it like sausage.

4. Twist both the ends. Steam the sausage for 5 minutes over boiling water.

5. Once steamed, remove the paper and heat the oil in a frying pan and cook the sausage until golden.

6. Serve immediately with tomato sauce or make hot dogs with mayonnaise and tomato sauce.

Gluten-free option: Use gluten-free tomato sauce and Worcestershire sauce. Replace the hot dog bun with a gluten-free version.

Serves 4

Potato Pie

Miso is the secret ingredient when making a 'bean-naise' sauce! This vegetarian version of a bolognese perfectly complements mashed potato and soy béchamel. You can easily impress your non-vegetarian friends with this dish, which I have done many times. This recipe is everybody's favourite.

Super easy béchamel
60g (2oz) glutinous rice flour (sweet rice flour)
600ml (21fl oz) soymilk
1 teaspoon MSG-free vegetable stock powder
²/₃ teaspoon sea salt
Pinch of nutmeg
Pinch of white pepper
Extra soymilk, for wash

Bean-naise sauce
150g (5oz) tomato paste
2 tablespoons red wine
1 tablespoon miso
½ teaspoon sea salt
1 teaspoon soy sauce
1 tablespoon olive oil, for frying
1 garlic clove, minced
½ onion, finely chopped
100g (3½oz) mushroom, finely chopped
60g (2oz) walnuts, finely chopped
1 tin (400g/14oz) red kidney beans

Mashed potato
850g (30oz) potatoes, peeled, coarsely chopped
120ml (4fl oz) soymilk
1 teaspoon sea salt
Pinch of white pepper

Garnish
2 tablespoons walnuts, chopped

1. Preheat oven to 180°C (350°F).

2. To make the mash, cook the potato in a large saucepan of water for 10 minutes or until tender. Drain and return to the pan. Use a potato masher to mash until smooth. Add the milk and stir until well combined. Season with salt and pepper.

3. To make the béchamel sauce, put glutinous rice flour into a bowl and add ¹/₃ of soymilk slowly. Mix very well with whisk. Gradually add the rest of the soymilk and mix.

4. Strain the mixture into a saucepan and heat over a medium heat. Add the stock powder, sea

salt, nutmeg and pepper, stir occasionally and cook until thick.

5.   To make bean-naise sauce, mix together the tomato paste, red wine, miso, sea salt and soy sauce ingredients then set aside.

6.   Heat oil in a large frying pan over a medium heat. Add garlic and onion and sauté until soft. Add mushroom and walnuts and cook until mushroom is soft. Add the sauce mixture. Cook until sauce thickens. Set aside.

7.   Spread the mash in a lightly greased ovenproof dish. Spread bean-naise sauce over the mash. Top with soy béchamel. Brush soymilk on béchamel. Sprinkle the chopped walnuts evenly over béchamel. Bake for 20 minutes or until golden. Serve.

Tip: I like to make double or triple portions of 'bean-naise' sauce and freeze. This sauce is extremely versatile so it is very handy to have in the freezer.

Gluten-free option: Make sure to use rice miso not barley miso.

Potato Pie

Unagi Donburi

Serves 4

Unagi Donburi

Eel bowl

In this recipe, you will be creating an eel-like texture with tofu and eating it with a typical eel sauce. Some people don't like eel because of the fishy smell, but of course the dish here is not fishy at all. Normally, we eat eel with white rice but I have used amaranth and millet to increase the nutritional value.

Eel
300g (10½oz) firm tofu
2 tablespoons potato, finely grated
1 tablespoon tapioca flour
Pinch of salt
1 sheet nori
2 teaspoons neutral oil

Sauce
60ml (2fl oz) mirin
20ml (½fl oz) sake
2 teaspoons unrefined sugar
70ml (2½fl oz) soy sauce

Mixed grain rice
1½ cup medium grain rice
¼ cup millet
¼ cup amaranth
2 cups water

Garnish
Sansyo pepper (optional)

1. Thoroughly get rid of excess water from tofu by boiling and let it stand for 10 minutes or if you don't boil it, let it stand with a heavy weight on top for at least two hours.

2. To make the sauce, place mirin and sake in a small pot, bring to the boil, and keep boiling for 1 to 2 minutes to get rid of the alcohol. Add sugar and soy sauce and simmer over a medium low heat for 5 minutes or cook until slightly thick.

3. To cook rice, wash the rice and grains.

4. Place washed rice, grains and water in a medium pot and put on a lid then bring to the boil. Reduce the heat and simmer for 10 minutes. Turn off the heat and let stand for 10 minutes.

5. To make eel fillet, place the tofu, grated potato, tapioca flour and salt in a food processor and process until smooth.

6. Place the tofu mixture onto the nori sheet and spread evenly.

7. Make lines on the surface with chopstick or knife to look like eel

8. Cut into 8 pieces.

9. Heat oil in a frying pan over a medium heat. Place the tofu slice with the nori side down.

10. Cook until golden colour and turn over to cook on the other side.

11. To serve, place the rice in a bowl then put 2 pieces of eel fillet on top, and pour on some sauce.

12. Sprinkle the sansyo pepper (optional) on top.

Gluten-free option: Use tamari instead of soy sauce.

Tempeh Nanbanzuke

Nanbanzuke is a Japanese version of the Spanish *escabeche* and contains soy sauce. Basically, you deep-fry and marinate the tempeh, and then serve it cold. This marinade is most popular with seafood; however, I use tempeh. Tempeh has a solid texture so it becomes a substantial main dish. Enjoy this sweet and sour dish.

2 medium onions, peeled and thinly sliced
3 carrots, peeled and thinly cut
2 packets (500g/17½oz) tempeh
Potato flour (starch), for dusting
Oil, for frying

Nanban marinade
160ml (5½fl oz) mirin*
4 tablespoons unrefined sugar
240ml (8½fl oz) rice vinegar
160ml (5½fl oz) soy sauce

1.   Pour boiling water over the sliced onion. Drain well.

2.   Transfer onion and carrot to a non-metallic dish in a single layer.

3.   To make marinade, place mirin and sugar in a small saucepan. Bring to the boil over a medium heat and mix well. Turn off the heat, then add vinegar and soy sauce. Set aside.

4.   Cut the tempeh in half lengthways, then cut into four rectangles to make 8 pieces in total.

5.   Toss tempeh lightly in potato starch and shake away excess. Heat oil in a saucepan over a high heat. When oil is hot, deep-fry tempeh until it is golden.

6.   Place the tempeh onto the onion and carrot and pour the marinade sauce over it while still hot.

7.   Cool to room temperature, then refrigerate for at least 2 hours or overnight.

Tip: You can also use celery or daikon (radish), instead of carrot and onion.

Gluten-free option: Use tamari instead of soy sauce.

Serves 4

Tempeh Teriyaki Burger

Fry tempeh with potato flour to add that extra 'fatty' taste, which substitutes for the meat fat. I still sometimes miss the taste of meat but I like this tempeh burger even more than a beef burger now.

1 tablespoon neutral tasting oil (for onion)
Salt, to taste
2 tempeh pieces
Potato flour (starch), for dusting
3 tablespoons neutral oil (for frying tempeh)
4 wholemeal burger buns
4 tablespoons egg-free mayonnaise
1 large onion, peeled and sliced
8 lettuce leaves, washed
2 tomatoes, sliced
Extra salt, to season tomato
Potato flour (starch), for dusting

Teriyaki sauce
2 tablespoons soy sauce
2 tablespoons mirin
1 tablespoon sake
½ tablespoon agave or natural sweet syrup

1.   Heat 1 tablespoon oil in a large frying pan over low heat. Add the onions and a pinch of salt and cook very slowly for 15–20 minutes, stirring occasionally to prevent them from catching. Cook until softened and golden. Set aside.

2.   To make teriyaki sauce, combine the teriyaki sauce ingredients and mix well. Set aside.

3.   Cut each tempeh into 2 pieces, making 4 pieces in total.

4.   Toss tempeh lightly in potato starch and shake away excess.

5.   Heat the oil in a frying pan over a medium heat, fry the tempeh until golden on both sides.

6.   Add the teriyaki sauce and bring to the boil. Reduce heat and simmer. Toss well to coat the tempeh completely with teriyaki sauce.

7.   To assemble, cut the burger buns in half. Spread the mayonnaise onto both sides.

8.   Place the base of each bread on serving plates. Top with lettuce, tempeh and tomato; sprinkle with salt and onion. Top with another bun. Serve immediately.

Gluten-free option: Use gluten-free buns and tamari instead of soy sauce.

Vegetarians, use whole egg mayonnaise or Japanese mayonaise.

Mains   167

Tofu and Tofu Skin Sausage

It is hard to imagine that you can make sausage using tofu and tofu skin—and it's tastier than you think. This sausage is amazing as it is or you can grill it just like real sausage.

100g (3½oz) dried tofu skin
2 tablespoons tamari
350g (12oz) hard tofu
1 tablespoon tahini
1 tablespoon sesame oil
120g (4oz) rice flour

1.   Soak the dried tofu skin in lukewarm water. When soft, drain.

2.   Place the tofu skin, with enough water to cover it, and tamari in a saucepan and cook over a medium heat until the liquid is almost gone (about 20 to 30 minutes).

3.   Place the tofu skin and all the ingredients into a food processor and process until smooth.

4.   Cut baking paper into an A4 size.

5.   Place ¼ of the mixture on the baking sheet and shape like a sausage. Then roll with paper. Twist both ends. Repeat for the rest of the mixture.

6.   Cover, place steamer over a saucepan of boiling water and cook for 20 minutes or until cooked. Set aside to cool.

Tip: Serve these sausages like you would meat sausages.

Try them in a wholemeal sandwich with avocado, alfalfa and baby spinach.

Or at breakfast, serve with some scrambled egg, grilled tomato, avocado and sautéed baby spinach.

Tofu Lasagna

Instead of pasta, make lasagna layers of grilled tofu and vegetables. With oven-baked tomato sauce, this dish is so simple and tasty and is the perfect way to enjoy this wonderful sauce.

300g (10½oz) firm tofu or silken firm
1 eggplant (aubergine), cut into thin rounds
2 zucchini (courgette), cut in half, then thinly sliced
Rice flour or potato flour (starch), to coat the tofu for dusting
Olive oil, for frying
Salt and pepper, to taste
150g (5oz) dairy-free mozzarella cheese, thinly sliced

Roasted tomato sauce

5 to 6 tomatoes (about 600g/21oz) cut in half
2 garlic cloves
1 large onion, peeled and sliced
1 small carrot (about 75g/2½oz), chopped
1 stalk celery (about 100g/3½oz), chopped
1 tablespoon dried oregano
60ml (2fl oz) olive oil
2 bay leaves
Salt and pepper, to taste
8 fresh basil leaves

Super easy gluten and dairy-free béchamel

60g (2oz) glutinous rice flour (sweet rice flour)
600ml (21oz) soymilk
1 teaspoon MSG-free vegetable stock powder
2/3 teaspoon sea salt
Pinch of nutmeg
Pinch of white pepper

1.   Place tofu on a tilted chopping board and let stand for 10 minutes.

2.   Cut the tofu in half lengthways and slice into 1cm thick pieces.

3.   Preheat the oven at 160°C (320°F).

4.   Line a baking dish with baking sheet.

5.   Place all ingredients for tomato sauce, except fresh basil, in a lined baking dish and toss to combine. Arrange tomato with the skin side is face up so after cooking you can remove the tomato skin easily.

6.   Bake for 45 minutes to 1 hour or until tomatoes are collapsed, skins are winkled and golden brown, and the juices are flowing.

7. Remove tomato skins and bay leaves with tongs. Cool down.

8. Meanwhile, pat the surface of the tofu with kitchen paper. Sprinkle salt and pepper on both sides of tofu.

9. Heat a chargrill pan over a high heat. Drizzle the eggplant, zucchini and tofu with the olive oil. Chargrill eggplant and zucchini in batches for 2 minutes each side, or until lightly charred and tender. Do the same with the tofu. Remove and set aside.

10. To make béchamel sauce, put glutinous rice flour into a bowl and add 1/3 of soymilk slowly—mix very well with a whisk.

11. Add the rest of soymilk and mix.

12. Strain the mixture into saucepan and heat over a medium heat.

13. Add the stock powder, sea salt, nutmeg and pepper, stir occasionally and cook until thick.

14. For the tomato sauce, place the roasted vegetables and basil in a blender or food processor and process until smooth. Season to taste.

15. To assemble the lasagna in 2 layers, spray a baking dish with oil. Spread 1/3 of tomato sauce over the base of the dish, top with vegetables, then 1/4 of the béchamel sauce.

16. Place 1/3 of the tomato sauce on top of that, to begin the second layer, followed by all the tofu. Finish the layer with the remaining béchamel and cheese. Place lasagna in a pre-heated oven at 180°C (350°F) and bake for 20 to 30 minutes.

Tip: This dish is a little bit runny compared to traditional lasagna. If you can cook this individually, in small baking dishes, it would be less messy. If you do it this way, you should be able to make 4 small baking dishes. For vegetarians, use pizza cheese or mozzarella.

Tofu Lasagna

Serves 4 as a main meal 6 as a starter

Tofu Ricotta Pasta

This is a fantastic way to enjoy tofu ricotta cheese. It's great to add parmesan cheese (preferably a non-dairy one) into this recipe to enjoy a more cheesy flavour.

400g (14oz) penne
1 large broccoli, cut into florets
80ml (2½fl oz) extra virgin olive oil
3 cloves garlic, crushed
1 punnet cherry tomatoes, cut in half
4 tofu ricotta (see the recipe for Tofu Ricotta), cut into small pieces
4 tablespoons parsley, chopped
1 tablespoon sea salt
Cracked black pepper

1.   Cook pasta in a saucepan of rapidly boiling water until it is al dente. Add the broccoli just before it has finished cooking to blanch.

2.   While pasta is cooking, heat oil and garlic in a large saucepan over a medium low heat until it becomes a light golden colour. Add tomato and sauté for 1 minute.

3.   Drain pasta and broccoli and add them to the garlic mixture with tofu ricotta cheese, parsley and salt.

4.   Toss to combine and serve with a generous sprinkling of black pepper.

Gluten-free option: Use gluten-free penne pasta.

Tofu Ricotta, Mushroom and Spinach Pie

I bet nobody but you will notice that there is tofu in this pie as the tofu ricotta will melt. Just make sure to season the tofu ricotta with salt and pepper for the best result. Please bake this pie for your tofu-hating friends.

1 bunch silverbeet (swiss chard), white stems removed, washed, with water clinging to the leaves
2 tablespoons extra virgin olive oil
400g (14oz) mushrooms, sliced
1 teaspoon sea salt
½ teaspoon nutmeg
4 sheets frozen ready-rolled puff pastry
4 tofu ricotta, sliced (see Tofu Ricotta recipe)
Extra salt, for seasoning ricotta
Cracked black pepper
Extra soymilk, for brushing

1.   Preheat the oven to 200°C (400°F). Line a baking tray with baking paper.

2.   Place silverbeet in a saucepan. Cover with a lid and cook over a low heat for 2 minutes or until wilted. Remove from heat. Set aside for 5 minutes to cool. Squeeze out any excess liquid.

3.   Heat the oil in a frying pan and add the mushrooms. Sauté until softened, and add the spinach, salt and nutmeg and sauté for a further 1 minute. Then set aside.

4.   Partially thaw pastry sheet just before baking.

5.   Cut each pastry sheet in quarters. Place on the sliced ricotta and season with salt and pepper. Then place spinach and mushroom on the pie sheet.

6.   Fold the sheet to close. Using a fork, press edges together to seal.

7.   Repeat with remaining pastry squares and fillings. Place on prepared tray. Brush pastry with soymilk.

8.   Bake for 15 to 20 minutes or until golden and puffed, then serve.

DESSERTS

Baked Apple with Sweet Potato Custard

Make rich and tasty custard with sweet potato and soymilk. Unlike traditional custard, there is zero cholesterol. Pumpkin can also be used in the custard, which is very yummy.

Custard
400g (14oz) purple skin sweet potato, peeled and
   cut into small pieces
400ml (14fl oz) soymilk
60ml (2fl oz) agave or pure maple syrup
½ teaspoon vanilla paste
2 tablespoons neutral taste oil
60g (2oz) glutinous rice flour
Pinch of salt

Apple
200g (7oz) sliced apples
2 tablespoons sultanas, soaked in brandy or
   Grand Marnier

Decoration
Some sliced almonds

1. Preheat the oven 200°C (400°F).

2. Place the potato in a saucepan and cover half of the potato with water.

3. Place the lid on and cook over a medium-low heat. When potato is nearly cooked, take off the lid and cook over a medium-high heat to evaporate the water (in this way, potato won't get watery but will bring out its sweetness).

4. Add the cooked potato, soymilk, maple syrup, vanilla paste, oil, rice flour and salt into a food processor and process until smooth.

5. Place the mixture back in the pot and cook over a medium-low heat until slightly thick (if you keep cooking, the texture gets hard, so do not overcook!).

6. Divide the sliced apple and sultanas between the ramekins (keep some apple for the decoration) then pour the custard over the top.

7.   Sprinkle over the sliced almond and add the rest of the apple.

8.   Bake in the oven for 15 to 20 minutes.

Tip: If you don't wish to use alcohol for kids, you can soak the sultanas in hot water.

You can make the custard with pumpkin. When you use pumpkin instead of sweet potato, reduce the amount of soymilk.

You can also bake this in one large baking dish. When you do, slice the apple thicker and bake for 30 minutes.

Baked Apple with Sweet Potato Custard

Green Tea Soy Custard

Green Tea Soy Custard

I love this custard. It's light, healthy and still very tasty. This is a popular dessert in my cooking class, especially among Asian people—they just love this. I put extra passion into this recipe to make it perfect. You will need to put soymilk and sugar into two different mixtures to bind the mixture more effectively.

Green tea mixture
1 tablespoon green tea powder
2 tablespoons unrefined sugar
2 tablespoons warm water

Mixture
700ml (24fl oz) soymilk
2 tablespoons unrefined sugar
½ teaspoon agar-agar concentrated powder
2 egg yolks

Black syrup
60g (2oz) real brown sugar
50ml (1¾fl oz) water

1. To make the green tea mixture, place green tea and sugar in a small bowl and mix well. Add the warm water slowly to mix. Set aside.

2. Heat half of the soymilk, all of the sugar and all the agar in a saucepan over a high heat, and bring to the boil. Reduce heat to low and simmer for at least 2 minutes. If you do not simmer agar in a boiling liquid for 2 minutes, it won't set. Make sure you stir and scrape the side of saucepan with spatula so as not to leave agar on the side (see the tip).

3. Place the egg yolks and the rest of the soymilk in a bowl and mix well. Add it to the mixture in a saucepan and mix. Then add the green tea mixture. Strain the mixture through a fine strainer.

4. Pour mixture into 4 small ramekins. Refrigerate for 1 hour or until set.

5. To make black syrup, heat the brown sugar and water in a small saucepan over a medium-high heat and bring to the boil. Reduce the heat to low and simmer for 2 minutes. Consistency is supposed to be still runny. It will become a syrup-like consistency when it cools down.

6. Serve the custard with black syrup.

Tip: This recipe uses a minimum amount of agar agar because I like this custard to be 'just set', meaning not fully solid.

Make sure you keep scraping the side of the pot and keep stirring. If you don't do that, most of the agar agar is left on the side of the pot. Or you can simply add a little extra agar.

There are a few types of agar agar—powder, flakes and bar. Their strength varies. If you use agar flakes or stick, put in four times more than the concentrated agar-agar powder (2 teaspoons).

If you use Japanese agar-agar powder, put two times more (1 teaspoon).

Vegan option: Simply omit the egg. Trust me, it is still nice. Also, omit egg and use 100ml (3½fl oz) condensed soymilk and 600ml (21fl oz) soymilk instead of using 700ml (24¾fl oz) soymilk. You can also omit 1 tablespoon of sugar when you boil the soymilk.

Both these ways are actually easier because you don't need to cook the soymilk separately. Simply cook all the soymilk (and soy condensed milk) and agar together and add the green tea mixture. Just make sure you cool down the soy mixture a little before adding the green tea mixture to avoid losing the beautiful green colour.

Mango Pudding

Unlike ordinary mango pudding, this is dairy-free and contains zero animal products like gelatine and cream. A little lemon juice intensifies the full flavour of the mango!

100ml (3½fl oz) water
100ml (3½fl oz) soymilk
2 tablespoons unrefined caster sugar
½ teaspoon concentrated agar-agar powder *
2 cups diced mango
2 teaspoons lemon juice

Garnish
Pieces of diced mango

1. Place water, soymilk, sugar and agar in a saucepan and bring to the boil. Reduce the heat and simmer for at least 2 minutes.

2. Place the mango in a blender and blend well. Add to the soymilk mixture and mix well.

3. Pour the mixture equally into four glasses and refrigerate until set and cool.

4. Serve with diced mango

Tip: If your mango is not fully ripened, add fresh orange juice instead of lemon juice or add extra sugar.

I like a soft texture so I add the minimum amount of agar agar powder. Ensure you scrape all the mixture from the side of the pot, with a silicon spatula; this way you will not miss any agar-agar when you stir.

If you use agar flakes or stick, put in four times more than the concentrated agar-agar powder (2 teaspoons).

If you use Japanese agar-agar powder, put two times more (1 teaspoon).

Okara Cookies

Okara cookies became really popular among Japanese girls who wanted to lose weight. When you eat dried okara and have some water, it expands in your stomach and keeps you feeling fuller for longer. Not only that, okara is also high in fibre and contains minerals and protein.

150g (5oz) okara
100g (3½oz) non-hydrogenated non-dairy butter*
80g (2½oz) unrefined sugar
100g (3½oz) sesame flour
20g (¾oz) cornflour (cornstarch)

1.   Preheat the oven to 130°C (265°F).

2.   To remove the water from okara, spread okara on a lined baking tray and bake for 30 minutes. Stir with a wooden spoon halfway through cooking. You want okara to weigh between 70g and 85g (2½–3oz) before you start. Take out the okara and allow it to cool down.

3.   Increase the oven temperature to 170°C (340°F).

4.   Place the okara in a food processor and process until fine.

5.   Place the butter and sugar in a bowl and whisk until creamy.

6.   Add the flour, cornflour and okara into the butter mixture and mix. Do not over mix.

7.   Shape into 2 logs and wrap them in plastic wrap. Refrigerate for 2 hours or until firm.

Remove and discard plastic wrap.

8.   Slice into 1cm-thick (½in) rounds. Place on trays and bake for 25 minutes or until golden. Transfer to a wire rack to cool.

Tip: You can dry the okara by cooking in a non-stick frying pan. Cook the okara in the frying pan over a medium heat and keep stirring with a wooden spoon for about 10 to 15 minutes.

If you use butter, soften the butter at room temperature, before adding the sugar.

It is very important to process the okara in a food processor to create a light and crunchy texture.

Okara Karintou
Okara stick

Traditionally a deep-fried Japanese sweet, this is an oven-baked version that adds okara for additional fibre and nutritional value.

4 tablespoons black sesame, roughly bruised
200g (7oz) okara
2 free-range eggs
200g (7oz) wholemeal flour
1 teaspoon baking powder

Coating sugar
4 tablespoons brown sugar (rapadura or panela*)
4 tablespoons water

1. Preheat the oven to 180°C (350°F). Line a baking tray with baking paper.

2. Bruise the black sesame with a knife or pestle and mortar.

3. Heat okara in a frying pan and cook over a medium-high heat for 5 minutes, to slightly reduce the amount of water. Allow it to cool down.

4. In a mixing bowl, whisk the eggs a little then add okara, flour, baking powder and black sesame.

5. Use a wooden spoon to stir until combined, then use your hands to bring the dough together in the bowl. Knead for 5 minutes or until smooth. You may need to add 1 teaspoon water if the dough is dry.

6. Place the dough in a plastic sandwich bag and roll it out to about 5mm thick.

7. Cut the edge of the bag to open.

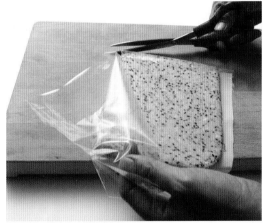

8. Cut into 5mm (¼in) strips and arrange on a lined tray.

9. Bake them for 20 minutes or until crispy.

10. To prepare the coating sugar, heat brown sugar and water in a frying pan and bring to the boil. Reduce the heat to low and simmer until thickened.

11. Add the sticks and mix well to make sure they are well-coated with sugar. Transfer to a lined baking tray to set.

Vegan option: Use 2 teaspoons of egg replacer and 4 tablespoons of water in a bowl instead of egg and whisk. Add the rest of the ingredients to combine.

Okara Karintou

Okara Kinako Cake

This recipe is made from beans—okara, azuki, soy beans and soybean powder—all beans. This cake will also make you feel full for longer and no oil or dairy are used.

1 tin (400g/14oz) cooked unsweetened
   azuki beans
1 tablespoon water
80g (2½oz) unrefined sugar (for azuki beans)
4 free-range eggs
100g (3½oz) unrefined sugar
200g (7oz) okara
Pinch of salt
80g (2½oz) kinako
1 teaspoon baking powder
Some soy vanilla ice-cream

1.   Preheat the oven to 180°C (350°F).

2.   Place azuki, water and sugar in a small pot and simmer for 15 minutes. Set aside to cool.

3.   Line the cake tin with baking paper.

4.   Place the eggs and sugar in the bowl and beat until light and creamy. Add the okara, 240g (8½oz) azuki and salt and mix well.

5.   Stir kinako and baking powder through the mixture and fold until just combined.

6.   Spoon the cake mixture into a prepared tin, and smooth the surface. Bake in a preheated oven for 30 minutes or until a skewer inserted into the centre comes out clean. Remove from oven.

7.   Cut into squares and serve with remaining azuki and ice-cream.

Vegan option: Instead of egg use 4 teaspoons of egg replacer and 160ml (5½fl oz) water. Place in a food processor and process until it is a little fluffy (or you can whisk).

Tip: Cooked sweetened azuki are available in cans but they are very sweet and cooked with a lot of refined sugar, so I recommend you cook them yourself with unrefined sugar. Since no oil is being used to sweeten them, cover the pot with foil while the beans are cooling, to avoid drying them out. When you store them, please cover with wrap.

Tofu and Berry Tiramisu

This recipe turns a decadent Italian dessert into a light, healthy and colourful masterpiece. It also gives you the perfect opportunity to use up your old bread!

10 wholemeal slices of bread, (cut the crust off and discard or to feed the birds!)

Tofu cream
3 packets of silken firm or pressed silken tofu (about 940g/33oz)
30ml (1fl oz) lemon juice
3 teaspoons vanilla paste
140ml (5fl oz) agave or pure maple syrup

Berry layer
250g (9oz) frozen mixed berries
3 tablespoons agave syrup or pure maple syrup

Garnish
1 punnet of your favourite fresh berries (optional)

1.   Boil the tofu to get rid of the water. Drain.

2.   Place tofu, lemon juice, vanilla and agave into a food processor and process until smooth.

3.   Make the berry layer by heating up the frozen berries and agave syrup in a medium sized saucepan over a medium heat and cook until completely defrosted. Strain the berry and keep the berry juice and berries separately.

4.   Using four slices of bread, dip each slice one at a time into the berry juice, turning to coat. Place, in a single layer, over the base of a 5cm-deep (2in), 18 x 18cm (7 x7in) (base) baking dish.

5.   Spread half the tofu cream over the bread to cover. Repeat layers with remaining bread and tofu cream. Cover and refrigerate for 2 hours.

6.   Top with the cooked berries that you set aside, and also the fresh berries.

Tip: You can use sponge finger biscuits if you don't have old bread. If you do that, add 2 tablespoons of water when you cook the frozen berries.

Gluten-free option: Use gluten-free bread.

Tofu Cheesecake

This cheesecake is delightfully rich and creamy without any dairy products—and it is also extremely nutritious.

Base
2 cups cashew nuts
2 tablespoons agave syrup
½ teaspoon vanilla paste
¼ teaspoon sea salt

Filling
900g (32oz) firm tofu
225ml (8fl oz) maple or agave syrup
85ml (2½fl oz) lemon juice
3 tablespoons kuzu
3 teaspoons vanilla paste
3 tablespoons neutral oil

1. Preheat oven to 170°C (340°F).

2. Line a 20cm (8in) base springform tin with baking paper.

3. Process cashew nuts to a fine meal. Add remaining ingredients until combined. Do not over process. You want the mixture to be crumbly. Press mixture over the base and sides of the prepared pan. Refrigerate.

Filling

1. Process all the ingredients until smooth.

2. Pour mixture into the prepared pan. Place pan on a baking tray.

3. Bake for 45 minutes to 1 hour or until just set (cheesecake will wobble slightly in centre). Turn off oven. Cool cheesecake in oven for 3 hours with door ajar. Refrigerate overnight.

Serves 6

Tofu Choco Banana

This is a really easy and nutritious dessert! Cooked banana works as a setting agent. The delicious and strong banana and coco powder neutralises the tofu taste, yet the tofu still delivers a rich and creamy texture.

300g (10½oz) banana flesh, sliced
300g (10½oz) silken tofu
25g (¾oz) pure cocoa powder
50ml (1¾fl oz) soymilk
30g (1oz) unrefined sugar

Garnish and filling
2 medium-sized bananas, peel and cut into
  1cm (½in) thick for filling and slice thinly for
  garnish
Some chervil leaves

1. Heat the sliced banana in a frying pan over a medium heat and cook until well mashed.

2. Place the tofu, cooked banana, cocoa powder, soymilk and sugar into the food processor and process until smooth.

3. Spoon half the tofu mixture into the bottom of the serving dish. Layer on the sliced banana. Top with the remaining tofu mixture. Refrigerate until cool.

4. To serve, garnish with thinly sliced banana and chervil leaves.

5. Alternatively, you can serve this in individual glasses. Spoon half the tofu mixture among six serving glasses. Place equal amounts of banana in each glass, spreading it over the tofu. Top each glass with the remaining tofu. Refrigerate until cool.

Tofu Chocolate Mousse

This one is for adults only. It has a strong, dark chocolate taste with rum. Coconut oil is the secret ingredient to set the mousse.

2 teaspoons coconut oil
30g (1oz) good-quality pure cocoa (use cocoa that has no sugar or milk powder added)
2 tablespoons agave syrup or other natural syrup
1 packet (300g/10½oz) silken tofu
¼ teaspoon rum essence

Garnish
1 punnet of strawberries

1. Place coconut oil, cocoa powder and agave syrup into a small saucepan over a medium heat until warmed through and shiny.

2. Add tofu and mix roughly. Heat until tofu is just warm.

3. Place tofu mixture and rum into a food processor or blender and mix until smooth.

4. Pour mixture into four ramekins, cover, and allow to set in the refrigerator for at least an hour.

5. Serve alone or topped with strawberries.

Tofu Shiratama Dango

Dumplings

You need only two ingredients for this recipe and it's so easy to make. Traditionally, we make dumplings without tofu; however, tofu makes these dumplings more nutritious and moist for longer. Use this basic recipe then serve with whatever flavour topping you desire.

300g (10½oz) silken tofu
230g (8oz) glutinous rice flour*

1.   In a medium bowl, mix together tofu and rice flour; knead until the mixture combines together to resemble dough. Form the tofu mixture into approximately 40 evenly sized balls.

2.   Carefully add the balls to a large saucepan of boiling water. To produce a perfect texture, cook for a further 2 minutes after all the dumplings have risen to the surface.

3.   In a colander, cool the dumplings under cold running water, gently rotating the balls from time to time to prevent them from sticking to one another. Drain well.

4.   Serve the dumplings with one or several of the following sweet or savoury variations.

Tip: The quantities specified in each of the variations, with the exception of Isobe Yaki, are sufficient for 20 dumplings (or to serve 4–5 people). Adjust the quantities where necessary to match the number of variations and dumplings being served.

Isobe Yaki

Soy sauce and nori

This is a popular way to eat rice cake (mochi); so why not do it with dumplings? The delicious smell and taste is created by slightly burning soy sauce!

40 Tofu Shiratama Dango (see recipe)
Soy sauce or tamari
Nori sheets, cut into squares

Garnish
Black sesame

1.   Preheat the grill to 180°C (350°F) (or medium heat).

2.   Place the dumplings on a lightly greased oven tray and grill close to the heat for 5 minutes or until the dumplings gently colour and appear slightly puffy.

3.   Liberally brush the surfaces of each dumpling with soy sauce.

4.   Put the dumplings back under the grill and cook for 1 minute.

5.   Remove dumplings and once more liberally brush the surfaces of each dumpling with soy sauce.

6.   To serve, position one cooked dumpling on a 3–4cm (1¼–1½in) square piece of nori and top with black sesame.

Isobe Yaki

Tofu Mitarashi Dango

Dango-skewered dumplings are a very popular Japanese sweet. It is a slightly grilled dumpling with a sweet soy-based sauce.

20 Tofu Shiratama Dango

Sauce
½ tablespoon potato starch
50ml (1¾fl oz) water
2 tablespoons soy sauce
1 tablespoons unrefined sugar
1½ tablespoons mirin

1. Thread dumplings onto 6 skewers. Place the skewers under the grill until dumplings turn a slightly brown colour. Alternatively, use a domestic blowtorch to get the colour.

2. Mix potato starch and water. Set aside.

3. Place 50ml (1¾fl oz) water, soy sauce, sugar and mirin in a small saucepan and bring to the boil.

4. Add the potato starch water (mix again just before adding, even though you mixed it earlier) into the boiling sauce and mix well. Cook until thickened.

5. Pour the sauce over the skewered dumplings.

Gluten-free option: Use tamari instead of soy sauce.

Serves 4

Zenzai

Warm red bean soup

This is another popular way to enjoy rice cake (mochi). It reminds me of Japanese New Year as my mother makes this every year on 1 January.

20 Tofu Shiratama Dango (see recipe)
1 x 425g (15oz) can cooked, undrained adzuki
60g (2oz) brown sugar*
Pinch of salt
100ml (3½fl oz) water

1.   Combine the adzuki, sugar, salt and water in a medium saucepan and bring to the boil over a medium heat, stirring occasionally.

2.   Reduce heat and add the dumplings, simmering gently for 5 minutes or until the dumplings are heated through.

3.   With a spoon or ladle, skim the foam from the surface of the mixture and discard. Place 2 or 3 dumplings into each small serving bowl.

4.   Spoon over the sauce and serve.

Black Syrup and Kinako

This is one of the most popular dumpling recipes in my cooking class.

20 Tofu Shiratama Dango (see recipe)

Black syrup
60g (2oz) rapadura or panela sugar
50ml (1¾fl oz) water

Kinako mixture
2 tablespoon kinako
2 tablespoon rapadura or panela sugar
Pinch of salt

1. To prepare the black syrup, bring the water and 30g (1oz) of brown sugar to the boil over a medium heat in a small saucepan.

2. Stirring continuously, reduce the heat and simmer for 2 minutes or until the syrup has slightly thickened.

3. Set aside to cool.

4. Combine the kinako, pinch of salt and 1 tablespoon brown sugar together.

5. Roll the dumplings into the mixture in order to coat well.

6. To serve, drizzle the black syrup over the kinako-coated dumplings.

Black Sesame and Maple Sauce

This sauce is also good to put on toast!

20 Tofu Shiratama Dango (see recipe)
2 tablespoons black tahini
2 tablespoons water
2 tablespoons maple syrup

1. Place all the ingredients in a small bowl and mix well.

2. Serve with dumplings.

Tofu, Cashew and Maple Ice-cream

This is a very rich and creamy ice-cream and it is really easy to make. The richness comes from the cashew nuts and tofu. It is a protein-rich ice-cream without the dairy and still tastes amazing. Cashews and maple are a wonderful combination!

600g (21oz) silken firm tofu
420g (15oz) unsalted cashew nuts
160ml/5½fl oz maple syrup

Garnish
cashew nuts, crushed
maple syrup

1.   Place all the ingredients, except tofu, in a food processor and process until smooth. Add tofu and process further.

2.   Place in a container with a lid and put in the freezer.

3.   Stir the mixture 2 hours later and freeze again until set.

4.   Serve with crushed cashew nuts and pour maple syrup over it.

Tip: If you can stir the mixture every 2 hours for three times, the outcome is even better.

Omega-3 Rich Apple Cupcakes with Tofu and Sweet Potato Cream

Flaxseeds and walnuts are rich in omega-3, which we often lack in our daily diet. Instead of sugary icing, use creamy sweet potato and tofu cream. These very nutritious sweets can even substitute for a meal!

200g (7oz) wholemeal flour
1 teaspoon baking powder
1 teaspoon cinnamon powder
½ teaspoon sea salt
30g (1oz) ground flaxseed
90ml (3fl oz) water
½ cup unsweetened apple sauce
80ml (2½fl oz) neutral oil
100g (3½oz) brown sugar or unrefined sugar
1 teaspoon vanilla extract
1½ apples (about 230g/8oz), peeled and chopped
100g (3½oz) walnuts, crushed

Sweet potato and tofu cream
120g (4oz) purple sweet potato
Pinch of salt
100g (3½oz) firm tofu
2 teaspoons maple syrup

Garnish
Cinnamon powder

1. Preheat the oven to 180°C (350°F).

2. Lightly grease a muffin tin or, alternatively, line holes with paper cases.

3. In a medium-size bowl, combine the flour, baking powder, cinnamon and salt.

4. In a mini food processor or small blender, whip the flaxseed and water together, until it reaches a thick and creamy consistency.

5. In a separate bowl, combine the apple sauce, oil, sugar, vanilla and flax mixture. Beat with an electric hand mixer or whisk until creamy smooth. Add to the flour mixture and stir until well blended. Do not over mix. If the mixture is too stiff, you can add 1 or 2 tablespoons of water or soymilk. The batter should be thick rather than smooth and wet, so please don't use too much liquid.

6. Fold in the apples and nuts.

7. Fill the greased muffin tins about three-quarters full.

8. Bake for 25 minutes or until cooked. You can check whether they are cooked using a wooden skewer inserted into the centre; if it comes out clean they're cooked.

9. Cool in tins for 5 minutes, then transfer to a wire rack to cool completely before icing.

10. To make sweet potato cream, peel the potato and boil with a pinch of salt until cooked.

11. Place the tofu, sweet potato, maple syrup and process until smooth. If the cream is too hard, add 1 or 2 teaspoons of soymilk.

12. Pipe the cream onto the apple cupcakes. Dust with cinnamon powder.

Tip: To use egg instead of flaxseed, whisk two eggs with sugar until pale then add apple sauce, vanilla and oil (process 4 and 5) and remove the water from the ingredients.

Blancmange

This is a rich and creamy blancmange that incorporates soymilk and tahini (the secret ingredient to make it really creamy). Japanese 'Kuzu' is the setting agent and it has many nutritional benefits. You can make noir (black) mange using black tahini.

2 tablespoons kuzu
500ml (17½fl oz) soymilk
60ml (2fl oz) agave
¼ teaspoon concentrate agar agar powder
2 tablespoons tahini

Strawberry sauce
30g (1oz) real brown sugar
25ml (¾fl oz) water
5 strawberries, chopped

1.   Break the kuzu into powder and dissolve with a small amount of soymilk in a saucepan.

2.   Add the rest of the soymilk, agave, agar agar and tahini over a medium heat, stirring continuously. You will see the mixture begin to thicken. Bring to the boil then turn down and simmer for 2 minutes, stirring continuously (agar agar needs to be cooked for at least 2 minutes with a boiling liquid, otherwise it won't melt so it won't set).

3.   Spoon the mixture among five ramekins and refrigerate to set.

4.   Meanwhile, make the strawberry sauce. Bring sugar and water to the boil in a small pan. Reduce heat to low and simmer until syrupy. Remove from heat and add the chopped strawberries and stir. Leave to cool.

5.   To serve, dip moulds briefly into warm water, turn onto plates and spoon strawberry sauce over the top.

Tip: There are many types of agar agar. If you use Japanese agar agar powder, use ½ teaspoon.

If you use an agar-agar flake or bar, use 1 teaspoon and soak for at least two hours before cooking.

You can also make black blancmange, simply use black tahini instead of white. You can also create the two-colour blancmange you see in the photo opposite.

Black Blancmange

Soy Scone with Tofu Cream

Soy Scone with Tofu Cream

I think that wholemeal flour is tastier than refined white flour. Having a warm scone with creamy yet light tofu cream is just heaven!

320g (11oz) wholemeal flour
50g (1¾oz) unrefined sugar
1 tablespoon baking powder
½ teaspoon sea salt
150g (5oz) non-hydrogenated non-dairy butter
30ml (1fl oz) water (if you use egg, please don't add this water)
120ml (4fl oz) soymilk
1½ tsp egg replacer (or 1 egg* see Tips)

Tofu cream
1½ pack silken firm or regular tofu (470g/16oz)
3 teaspoons lemon juice
1½ teaspoon vanilla paste
60ml (2fl oz) agave syrup

1. Place tofu on a tilted chopping board and let stand while preparing scone.

2. Preheat the oven to 220°C (420°F). Line a baking tray with baking paper. Position oven rack in the top half of the oven.

3. In a large bowl, combine the flour, sugar, baking powder and salt. Add the butter to the dried ingredients. Using fingertips, rub butter into flour mixture until mixture resembles fine breadcrumbs.

4. In a food processor or by handwhip the egg replacer and water until thick and creamy. Set aside.

5. Make a well in the centre of the mixture. Add soymilk and egg replacer mixture (if you use egg, add the beaten egg). Using a flat-bladed knife, stir just until dry ingredients are moistened. (You may need to add just 1 teaspoon of soymilk or water). Keep the mixing to a minimum to avoid developing the gluten in the flour, which will give you tough scones.

6. Turn out onto a lightly floured surface. Knead gently until just smooth.

7. Using a lightly floured rolling pin, gently roll dough out until 2cm (¾in) thick. Using a 6cm (2½in) round cutter, cut out scones. Press leftover dough together. Repeat this process to make 10 scones.

8. Place scones, just touching, on prepared tray. Bake for 15 to 20 minutes or until golden and hollow when tapped on top.

9. Meanwhile, make tofu cream. Place all the ingredients in a food processor and process until smooth.

10. Serve the warm scones with tofu cream.

Tip: If you use egg, beat the egg first then add to the butter and flour mixture with soymilk.

Don't twist the cutter when cutting out rounds. Push the cutter straight down into the dough, pressing down evenly—this helps the scones to rise.

Glossary

AGAR: Agar or agar agar (kanten in Japanese) is a vegetarian gelatin substitute produced from a combination of seaweed. It has been mostly used as an ingredient in desserts throughout Asia. It is white, semi-translucent and tasteless and comes in flakes or bars and also in a white powder. It dissolves in hot liquid and sets at room temperature.

The level of concentration of agar varies from brand and country of origin. Follow the manufacture's instruction as to the amount of liquid required although I put some suggested quantities for a few types of agar agar for the recipes.

AGAVE NECTAR: Pronounced 'ah-gah-vay', this natural sweetener comes from the blue agave plant that is similar to aloe or a cactus plant, and is found primarily in southern Mexico. This liquid is sweeter than honey or sugar.

Agave nectars are sold in light, amber, dark varieties. Light agave nectar has an almost neutral flavour and is therefore sometimes used in delicate-tasting dishes and beverages. Amber agave nectar has a medium-intensity caramel flavour and dark agave nectar has stronger caramel notes and a distinct flavour. It is available from health food shops.

AMARANTH: This is a highly nutritious gluten-free grain. It has been cultivated for 8,000 years and is an important food source for ancient civilisations in South America and Mexico.

AONORI: A type of seaweed, literally means 'green nori' or 'blue nori' and also known as aosa. This aromatic green seaweed is commonly dried and sold in flakes. They are used as a garnish for many Japanese dishes such as okonomiyaki, yakisoba and takoyaki and added to tempura batter. It is also used for sweets (ohagi) and rice crackers. Raw aonori is becoming popular in Japan.It is available in a dried form in Asian supermarkets.

ARAME: A type of edible black seaweed and a member of kelp family. It is used in Asian, especially Japanese cuisine. It is sold dried and chopped into string-like threads or strips because it is so tough in its natural form. It looks similar to the black seaweed, 'hijiki'. Before being packaged, both arame and hijiki are dried and then boiled, and then dried again.

Arame needs to be soaked before it is added to cooking. It does not take a long time to reconstitute (about 5 minutes) and it usually doubles in size. It has a milder flavour (hijiki is considered to have strong seaweed smell) and is more versatile. It can easily substitute for hijiki, which is a much more popular seaweed in Japan. But some countries no longer import hijiki, as it has been found to contain high levels of inorganic arsenic. Arame is available in health food stores.

AZUKI: Azuki is a transliteration of the native Japanese name for aduki beans. They are small, reddish-brown beans with a cream-coloured seam that are originated in China. It is particularly popular in Asian cooking, especially desserts. They are enjoyed boiled with sugar and mashed into a sweet red bean paste that is used as a filling in many popular Asian desserts. It also used in savoury dishes. Available as dried whole beans or tinned and cooked with or without sugar.

Azuki is available from Asian grocers or health food shop.

BENI SYOUGA: Red pickled ginger. Literally this means 'red ginger' in Japanese. Ginger is cut into thin strips and pickled in *umezu* (plum vinegar), the by-product of *umeboshi*, the salted japanese plum. It is quite often served with beef bowl, okonomiyaki (Japanese savoury pancake) and yakisoba (Japanese fried noodle).

BUTTER NON-DAIRY NON-HYDROGENATED: Non-dairy butter is technically margarine but most varieties contain trans-fat, which contributes to heart disease. That is why I choose non-dairy non-hydrogenated (means no trans fat) butter. In some countries, it can be hard to find, but look in health food shops or check the labels.

CHIA SEEDS: A super food that is rich in omega-3, antioxidant, protein and fibre, chia seeds are edible tiny seeds that come from the desert plant, a member of the mint family that grows abundantly in southern Mexico. They have the unique property of absorbing liquid and when soaked, they form gel. Black and white seeds are available.

They are available from health food shops

DAIKON: A mild-flavoured crunchy East Asian big white radish, originally from China. Unlike other radishes, it is as good cooked as it is raw.

The word daikon comes from two Japanese words: *dai* (meaning large) and *kon* (meaning root). Daikon are an important part of Japanese cuisine and can be eaten in many ways—raw, pickled, simmered, stir-fried and dried, then simmered.

The flavour is slightly different depending on the part of the root. The top thickest part of the root is sweeter and best used raw. The bottom part of the root is more pungent and is good for stir-frying and simmering, pickling or grating as a condiment for oily dishes such as tempura, grilled oily fish or even steak.

kuzu

nigiri flakes

seaweed

umeboshi

kinako powder

mixed grains

azuki beans

agar

aburage

have an egg allergy. Store ground flaxseeds in the fridge or freezer. As flaxseeds are an unsaturated fat, unless they are stored in an air-tight container in a fridge they can go rancid quickly.

They are available from health food shops.

DASHI POWDER/GRANULES: Dashi means stock in Japanese and considered fundamental to Japanese cooking. Dashi is the base for miso soups, clear broth soups, noodle broths, and many simmering dishes. The most common form of dashi is made by boiling kombu (edible kelp) and bonito flake and then straining the resultant liquid. Other kinds of dashi stock are made by kelp, shiitake, or niboshi (dried anchovy). These days, instant dashi powder or liquid is popular in Japan, the same as chicken stock is in Western countries. For vegetarians and vegans, kelp and shiitake mushroom dashi is great although most kelp or mushroom stock powder contains bonito. Many also contain MSG so please read the label carefully to choose the right one for you.

Available from Asian groceries or health food shops.

GLUTINOUS RICE FLOUR: Also, known as sweet rice flour. It is ground from short-grain glutinous rice, also known as 'sticky rice' that is very common in Asia. Even though it is gluten-free, it is called glutinous because of being glue-like or sticky. The chewy, elastic quality of the dough makes it a popular base for the creation of sweets throughout Asia. It is available from Asian groceries and some supermarkets.

KONBU: Type of edible seaweed that is also known as kelp. Konbu is large, flat and dark brown seaweed that is one of the main basic dashi ingredients in Japan.

When harvested and dried naturally, kombu acquires a thin layer of white powder that is extremely flavourful and should not be washed off. Konbu is commonly sold dried.

Some countries don't import konbu, so substitute with konbu instant dashi powder.

KUZU: A superior healthy starch with a smooth texture and neutral flavour that is naturally extracted from the roots of the kuzu plant.

Kuzu has been praised for its medicinal properties in China and Japan for thousands of years. When you buy kuzu, the powder will be in small chunks. Use it to thicken soups and stews, sauces, gravy and many types of desserts. Some kuzu contains potato starch so please look at ingredients carefully.

It is available from health food shops or Asian supermarkets.

MILLET: Millet is one of the oldest foods known to humans and provides various minerals. It is considered to be one of the most digestible grains. This tiny round grain has a sweet nutty flavour that has similar texture to couscous when cooked. Unlike most grains, millet is alkalising to the body.

Millet comes in several varieties and can be white, gray, yellow or red. This gluten-free, protein-rich grain is great for vegetarians and people who are gluten intolerant.

Available from health food shops.

MIRIN: Known as Japanese sweet rice wine, it is used only for cooking and not as a beverage. Mirin is a sweet-flavoured liquid, made from steamed glutinous rice, rice koji (the cultured grain in Japanese) and alcohol. The sweetness comes naturally when rice is cooked and mixed with koji. However, mirin-style seasoning, also known as low-alcohol mirin, is just syrup with seasoning and has 1 per cent alcohol, whereas real mirin contains 14 per cent. Real mirin is much healthier and tastier. It is available from supermarkets or Asian grocers.

NATURAL SWEETENER: Swap your refined sweetner with a natural sweetner. There is an array of natural sweetners to choose from including: agave syrup, rice syrup, raw honey, pure maple syrup, palm sugar and rapadura (panela) sugar.

NIGARI: A by-product of manufacturing salt from seawater. It is used to coagulate soy protein to make traditional Japanese tofu while Chinese-style tofu uses calcium sulfate for coagulation. Its main constituent is magnesium chloride. It is the Japanese name for a bitter salt as it has a bitter taste. It is available in powder, flake and liquid form.

It is available from health food shops and Asian supermarkets.

NORI: A type of edible seaweed. It is formed like paper sheets, compressed and dried. It is sold dried or toasted in sheets and available in different shapes such as square sheets, small rectangles or shredded. Seasoned nori (ajituke nori) is also available.

Nori sheets are used to roll around rice (sushi or rice ball) or vegetables and finely shredded nori is used as a topping or condiment for various noodles, pasta and salad.

OKONOMIYAKI SAUCE: Special sauce for okonomiyaki (Japanese savoury pancake). It is like worcestershire sauce or barbecue sauce, but thicker and sweeter. It is also commonly used for takoyaki (octopus ball) or fried noodle like yakisoba or yaki udon. Tonkatsu sauce (special sauce for deep-fried pork cutlets) has a very similar taste so you can buy either of them.

QUINOA: Pronounced 'keen-wah', it is a staple of the ancient Incas and was already cultivated more than 5000 years ago. Quinoa looks like a grain; however, it is actually a seed that originates from the cousin of the spinach plant. Quinoa has a complete protein unlike most plant food and is high in iron, magnesium, b vitamins and fibre. It has a chewy yet light and tender texture when cooked.

It is available from health food shops and supermarkets.

RAMEN: These Japanese noodles actually originated in China. Ramen is made from wheat flour, salt, water, and sometimes kansui, which is essentially a type of alkaline mineral water. Kansui gives yellow colour to the noodle. In some ramen noodles, egg is added instead of kansui.

Ramen comes in various shapes and lengths. It may be thick or thin, as well as straight or wrinkled. It is available fresh and dried from Asian supermarkets.

REAL BROWN SUGAR: Unrefined brown sugar, such as rapadura sugar. Many brown sugar producers produce brown sugar by adding cane molasses to completely refined white sugar crystals in order to reduce manufacturing costs. Rapadura sugar is when the sugar cane is juiced and then dehydrated over low heat. There are no other processes that happen—it is not cooked on a high heat and no chemicals or anti-caking agents are added. Because rapadura is not separated from the molasses, it has more nutrients, vitamins and minerals. *Rapadura* is the traditional name in brazil where it is produced. It is also known as panela, raspadura, chancaca or piloncillo—depending on where it has been made.

There are similar products to rapadura, such as Sucanat™ (available in the USA) and jaggery (India). In the process of producing sucanat, the sugar stream and the molasses stream are separated from each other during processing, then reblended to create a consistent product. Jaggery is whole cane sugar which has been heated to higher temperatures.

Muscavado, turbinado, demarara and 'organic raw sugar' are all refined, although not as much as white sugar

SAKE: Japanese rice wine. This wine is not just the Japanese national drink, but also an important ingredient in Japanese cookery. Sake is made from rice, koji (as a fermenting agent) and water. In its undiluted form, it has an alcohol content of around 15 to 20 per cent. Its characteristic aroma gives many dishes their special flavour, also bringing out the flavour of other ingredients.

Cooking sake is also available, which has added salt and other ingredients and is not suitable as an alcoholic drink.

SANSYO: Also known as Japanese pepper. It has an aromatic, tangy flavour without being hot. It produces a tingling and buzzing sensation and is similar to szechuan pepper.

It is actually not related to peppercorn. It is the ground dried leaves of the prickly ash tree and is commonly used for unagi (eel).

Sansyo is available from Asian supermarkets.

SHICHIMI TOUGARASHI: Traditional seasoning from Japan. *Tougarashi* is chilli and *shichi* is seven in Japanese, hence the name means 'seven flavour chilli' because seven ingredients are generally used, although ingredients vary according to the region.

Typical ingredients are red chilli pepper, roasted orange peel, white and black sesame seeds, Japanese pepper, nori and ginger. It is commonly used for noodle dishes, hot pot, tempura and yakitori (skewered chicken). It is available from Asian supermarkets.

SHIITAKE MUSHROOM: Native Japanese mushroom. Shiitake mushrooms are a symbol of longevity in Asia because of their health-promoting properties. Extracts from the mushroom, and sometimes the whole dried mushroom, are used in herbal remedies. Both fresh and dried shiitake are available. Dried shiitake must be reconstituted by soaking in water before using. Soaked water can be used as stock. Many people prefer dried shiitake to fresh, because umami flavour is produced by drying mushrooms.

Shiitake mushrooms are available from supermarkets.

SUSHI VINEGAR: Pre-mixed vinegar to make sushi rice. Sushi vinegar is made of rice vinegar, sugar, salt, and occasionally kombu and sake.

UDON: Udon are thick, white, wheat noodles, which are made by kneading wheat flour, salt and water. Dried, pre-boiled, and fresh udon are available at supermarkets. To cook udon noodles, following the package instructions works best since cooking time varies between brands.

UME/PLUM VINEGAR: A by-product of umeboshi. Fresh unripe *ume* (Japanese plum) are sundried several times until they've softened, then packed in barrels with sea salt covered by weight. Through the action of salt and pressure, the plums begin to shrink, and their juice starts to collect at the bottom of the barrel. This salty, sour liquid is called plum vinegar although it is not a true vinegar.

It is available from health food shops.

UMEBOSHI: Sun-dried and salted ume fruits with red shiso leaves (perilla), which are one of the most popular pickles in Japan. *Umeboshi* literally means 'dried plum' although it is actually a species of apricot.

This ancient Japanese health food tastes salty and extremely sour. Despite its strong acid taste, it is known as 'the king of alkaline foods'.

They are eaten as a condiment, often served with rice or used to make dressings and sauces for pasta or vegetable, tofu, meat and fish dishes.

It is available from health food shops or Asian grocers.

WAKAME: A type of edible seaweed that has a curly leaf and is dark green or brown in appearance. It has a mild flavour and soft texture and is commonly used in salads and soup. It can be purchase either dried or fresh, although the dried type is the most common, and are sold in pieces or flakes. The dried wakame expands when reconstituted either by soaking in water for a few minutes or adding directly to a soup.

WASABI: Also known as Japanese horseradish, although it is a root plant and not actually from the horseradish species of plants. Wasabi root is used as a condiment and has a sharp and fiery flavour that stimulates the nasal passages more than the tongue.

Wasabi is widely available as a paste or in powder form. Wasabi powder has to be mixed with water to become a paste. Fresh wasabi can be found but it is much more expensive and harder to get compared to tube and powder form.

It is available from Asian supermarkets.

Acknowledgements

I couldn't have completed this book without the great support of the people around me—I am extremely lucky to know such wonderful people. There are too many to mention here by name, but I would love to thank everyone who has helped, from when the book was just a dream to the actual work involved in making it.

Thank you very much to New Holland Publishing who has given me such a wonderful opportunity. Publishing my own cookbook has been a dream of mine for over a decade now, and I believed that when I was ready, the offer would come. Thank you especially to Lliane Clarke and Jodi De Vantier for letting me do the book the way I wanted.

A very grateful thank you too for the care and support from family in Japan and Ireland—especially for Catherine, who gave me constant consideration and encouragement, and for my mum, dad and sister in Japan who supported me doing what I love to do.

A very special thank to Sherly Susan, my fabulous photographer, for her patience and dedication, ability to work to a tight schedule and be able to handle my fussy requests for perfection. She is also a true friend who has always been there for me. Thanks also to her husband, Lukas, for his help and solid support with the photography and editing.

Thank you Rie Sakata for being such a talented assistant and helping me with everything from developing recipes to cooking dishes for the shoot. Thanks also for remembering the small things that helped support the Healthy Soy Cooking classes during very hectic times.

I'd like to thank to Kerry Hayes for his support of the Healthy Soy Cooking business in its early days. I started the cooking school in 2007. I had been teaching cooking since 1997 but after 10 years I really wanted to teach in my own way, with my own purpose and style. Thank you so much Kerry for all your support and encouragement—without your help, Healthy Soy Cooking wouldn't have happened.

Thanks to everyone who has come to a class. Special thank you also to those of you who are vegetarian or vegan; it was because of you that I started to think differently about food and what is truly possible when eating healthily as a vegetarian or vegan. Tao friends who keep supporting me with my vegetarian journey and providing me with new plants and ideas on a regular basis. It has been such a difficult journey to experiment with the vegetarian way, as my love of all kind of food has been so strong. I am still working on this but have certainly become healthier on this journey because of such great friends.

Also thank you to Hideo Dekura-san for being extremely kind with his time and his great advice, from someone who has already published many cookbooks.

Thank you also Julia Powel for reading all the legal documents and giving me sound advice—I appreciate your generosity; Ikuko Yamaoka, for giving me your warm support and marketing ideas for this book; and Nicola Comparin for tasting dishes and always giving honest feedback and valuable suggestions.

Thank you also to James Wilson from Spiral foods. We are lucky to have access to quality and genuinely healthy Japanese ingredients; this is because of James's passion in bringing quality Japanese food to the wider public in Australia. It has been fantastic to be able to use Spiral Foods' genuine healthy ingredients for my cooking classes and this cook book.

The same goes to Tsuyoshi Kiyosue san from Carwari again for providing genuine and high quality products for my classes and this book.

Thank you Terry Iwata san from Noritake Australia who provided me with such beautiful porcelain during the creation of this book. As a Japanese person I feel privileged to use Noritake dishes as I have been aware of their perfection, craftsmanship and elegant design since I was young.

Also thank you to Ian Woodhouse and Blanco Australia who let me use their fabulous kitchen for the photo shooting and cooking classes. It was so easy to do all the cooking with such an abundance of kitchen appliances.

Lastly and most importantly, thank you to Ronan Powell. Not only for the tremendous impacts he has made in my life, but also for being the fabulous, fun and sweet human being that he truly is. I recently achieved four long-held dreams that I have had for over 10 years; I achieved all of these since I met him. This book is one of them.

He has given me never-ending inspiration and tremendous support for this book in so many ways, physically, mentally, everything! I could not have gotten through this without his huge support. Thank you for being loving, caring and strong, for inspiring me, and for dreaming with me, for believing in me and for jumping in to save the day again and again and AGAIN!

Arigato gozaimasu!
Yoshiko Takeuchi

A very special thanks

A special thank you to Tetsuya Wakuda who gave me my real introduction to the world of excellence in cuisine, and also the opportunity to become the best I can be with food in terms of both quality and innovation.

Tetsuya is my mentor and he has the utmost discipline and caring for others, with genuine talent in what he does.

I had heard about Tetsuya while living in Japan and his great ability as a top-level chef, having won the title of 'Best Chef in Australia' for three years in a row. A year and three months later I was an apprentice in his kitchen.

Since I met Tetsuya, he encouraged and inspired me with his many wonderful words of wisdom and genuine caring, which helped me to grow so fast, and to this day his advice and teachings have stayed with me and have been a major help for my own development and modest successes.

This book is my attempt to apply what I learned from my mentor Tetsuya; it is my application of his teachings and attitude, within my own style, dreams and values.

Sincerely, thank you Tetsuya-san. Thank you for being so inspirational and a man of integrity and genuine talent.

One day, I would love to give back somehow, and I hope that this contributes in some way towards the world being an even better place for you, whether it be for your life, your mentorship for others or even your own healthy living.

Recipe index